Prayers for
Contemporary Worship

Prayers for
Contemporary Worship

THE SAINT ANDREW PRESS: EDINBURGH

First published in 1977 by
THE SAINT ANDREW PRESS
121 George Street, Edinburgh

On behalf of the Church of Scotland
Committee on Public Worship and Aids to Devotion

ISBN 0 7152 0351 7

Second impression 1979

Printed in Great Britain by Morrison & Gibb Ltd
and bound by Open Flat Bookbindings (Scotland) Ltd

CONTENTS

FOREWORD

This book represents a modest contribution towards the quest for prayer language which is contemporary but which avoids theological reductionism; language appropriate to a salvation which is in time but which is not time-bound.

The Committee on Public Worship and Aids to Devotion is grateful to the members of the small Sub-Committee under the convenership of the Rev. Kenneth Hughes who have produced this material, and commend it to the attention of the Church.

Andrew Stewart Todd

Convener, Committee on Public Worship and Aids to Devotion

INTRODUCTION

The task entrusted to the sub-committee responsible for
this volume was that of 'gathering, composing,
evaluating and editing prayers in the modern idiom'.
No attempt at definition of 'the modern idiom' was
made at the beginning of the exercise. Indeed, we do
not believe that there is one universally applicable
modern English idiom. We think, however, that it
may be useful to offer some reflections on the nature
of the language of public prayer for the consideration
of those who may turn to this volume for help with the
marshalling of prayers for congregational worship.

GENERAL CONSIDERATIONS

If the Church's worship is to be real and living, those
who lead it will require to use language with which
those who are worshipping with them can
honestly associate themselves. The search for a language
'understanden of the people' is one for which those
who stand in the tradition of the Reformation may be
expected to have a ready sympathy, but it is not the
sole consideration. The contemporary liturgist needs to
echo the words which a contemporary theologian
(Ronald Gregor Smith) reiterated in the margin of his
notes for his last book: 'Transcendence is what I must
concentrate on.' The language of worship must
help to point men and women significantly beyond
themselves. It must appeal, furthermore, not only to
the intellect, but also to the imagination, to the
emotions, to the will. It is no easy task to give
adequate weight to all of these considerations

simultaneously, and we do not suppose that the prayers which follow have succeeded in doing so more than occasionally, if at all.

SENTENCE CONSTRUCTION

Much traditional language is, in effect, translation English. For instance, the use of a vocative followed by a relative clause (O God, who hast . . .) is not a natural English construction but is almost universally used in Cranmer's translations or paraphrases of medieval Latin collects. From there its use has spread, and it is very widely employed as a means of setting forth the grounds on which a certain petition is made. It is interesting to note that Knox tends to use the more natural English form: 'O God, seeing that such and such is the case, we make such and such a request'. (We are not suggesting that, in general, we should go back to Knox rather than Cranmer!) It has been our endeavour to use sentence forms which are usual at the present day, but, because prayer spoken on behalf of a congregation is a kind of public speech it must sometimes have a certain declamatory quality about it. We do not believe that 'contemporary' is to be equated with 'casual' or 'conversational'.

VOCABULARY

It is not difficult to avoid the merely archaic (e.g. 'vouchsafe' and 'beseech'), and we hope we have succeeded in doing so. There are, however, certain other words, as alien to every-day vocabulary, such as 'amen' and 'alleluia' which there is a good case for retaining on the ground that they do point in the direction of 'significant mystery'. Then there is a considerable range of words (e.g. 'righteousness' and 'redemption') which were originally borrowed from secular vocabulary but which now have come to have technical religious meanings. It is a more difficult

question whether the unfamiliarity of such words is a
consideration of greater weight than their usefulness.
Pastoral considerations must be allowed to apply in
particular situations. It will be found that there has
been no attempt to exclude such words from this book.
At the same time it has been our endeavour to move
in the direction of doing for our day what the early
church did in a wide-ranging way—that is, to borrow
from the market-place words which we hope will be
spiritually illuminating. We believe that it is just as loyal
to scripture as our standard to borrow the scriptural
method of vocabulary building as merely to lift words
and phrases from the Bible. To put the matter
otherwise, we hope sometimes to have succeeded in
translating scriptural images and not merely in using a
modern translation of biblical words.

'YOU' AND 'THOU'
The tacit assumption is often made that only the 'you'
form of addressing Almighty God can be acceptable in
a collection of contemporary prayers. The Committee
is not convinced that such an approach to God in
itself guarantees either fresh language or unerring
insight. The contemporary nature of prayer does not
rest on such a simple mechanical rule. Some of the
material included, therefore, (notably I.7, II.1.i,
II.1.ii, II.1.iii, and II.1.iv) adopts the more traditional
form of 'thou', partly because it was submitted in this
form, and partly because the sentiments embodied in
such prayers, though couched in traditional language,
did not seem to be in any way outworn. It is felt that
prayers in 'thou' form (particularly those in section II)
do not readily lend themselves to conversion into the
more modern 'you'. However, there is not quite the
same difficulty in reverse, and it will be found that, if
desired, certain services in section I (2, 6, 8, and 9
particularly) transpose fairly readily into 'thou' forms

without great disruption of the rhythm and phrasing of the text.

OTHER WORK IN THIS FIELD

We are aware that our work is not of a pioneering nature. A considerable number of collections have already been published. Since, however, it appears that many of those responsible for the conduct of public worship who would like to use contemporary language are not fully aware of what is available, it has been represented to us that it might be useful to have a conspectus of some of the work most likely to be useful in Scottish parishes.

An early major collection of such material to be published was *Contemporary Prayers for Public Worship*, edited by Caryl Micklem, published by S.C.M. Press in 1967. Seven people contributed to this collection, and it contains some variety of style and language. When first published, it represented something of a breakthrough and was warmly welcomed. Some parts of it have stood up to constant use better than others. In particular, some of the prayers were thought to be too didactic. This collection remains, however, of great value and we would specially welcome its success with Adoration, which has so often defeated those seeking to produce prayers in contemporary language. It includes prayers for the seasons of the Christian year, and a great deal of useful material for the Great Prayer at the Lord's Supper. There is an excellent funeral service and some suitable material for use at marriage services, but the baptismal service will probably be found less useful within the Church of Scotland.

A sequel to this collection, called *More Contemporary Prayers* and prepared by some of the same people, seems to many less successful than the first collection. The didactic tendency already mentioned seems to have been given fuller rein in this second collection, and many of the prayers tend to sound more like sermons. There is, however, much that is valuable, and some material that is excellent. A recent third volume with the same editor, *Contemporary Prayers for Church and School*, has avoided some of the errors of the second.

A collection which has aroused considerable interest is *Your Word is Near*, the translation of prayers by a Dutch Jesuit, Huub Oosterhuis. This collection was published in the United States and is not widely available in this country. It can, however, be found in some Roman Catholic bookshops. As might be expected, it includes some material which would be unsuitable for use in the Church of Scotland. Distinctively Roman Catholic material forms, however, only a tiny proportion of a large and excellent collection. Oosterhuis is clearly a poet, and some of his phrases might not sound well on the lips of others. All the same, his collection contains a great deal of excellent material, including some very good prayers for Intercession.

Worship Now is a collection of services and prayers for public worship, mainly in contemporary language, first published by The St Andrew Press in 1972 and reprinted. The various prayers were contributed by a large number of people, and the compilers did not edit or alter the work that was sent to them. This collection, therefore, is very varied but it contains material which is proving extremely useful.

Alan Gaunt has published *New Prayers for Worship* in loose-leaf form (John Paul the Preacher Press). It contains much sensitive material of general usefulness. Two supplements have so far been published. As well as forms for sacraments and ordinances, the first of these contains a useful series of theme prayers ('collects') for the Christian Year based on the Calendar and Lectionary of the Joint Liturgical Group.

In 1970 three American Presbyterian Churches produced *The Worshipbook*. This contains orders of service for public worship entirely in contemporary language. Here, too, is a great deal of material that will be found very useful in the public worship of the Church of Scotland.

The 1973 edition of the B.B.C. publication *New Every Morning* contains some fairly successful rewriting of traditional material in 'you' form. This is a good quarry for short prayers on specific themes, perhaps rather conservative.

The work of the International Consultation on English Texts may not be as well known as it should be. This body includes representatives of the main Protestant Churches and representatives of the Roman Catholic Church, and has produced contemporary translations of the historic prayers of the Church, including the Lord's Prayer, the Apostles' Creed, the Nicene Creed, and the prayers traditionally associated with the Lord's Supper. These have been collected in a pamphlet called *Prayers we have in Common*, published by S.P.C.K.

The Committee's own recent publication *The Divine Service* includes an order for the celebration of the Lord's Supper using contemporary language. This publication is commended to the Church by the General Assembly, and has already found a wide acceptance.

Other useful material in contemporary language will be found in some of the official liturgical publications of the Church of England, and Roman Catholic Church in English-speaking countries.

NOTE: *Words printed in italics may be said by minister and people.*

I

COMPLETE SETS OF PRAYERS
FOR SUNDAY WORSHIP

Service 1

CALL TO PRAYER
God was in Christ, reconciling the world to himself, no longer holding men's misdeeds against them; and he has entrusted us with the message of reconciliation.

There is one Body and one Spirit, one Lord, one Faith, one Baptism; one God and Father of all, who is over all, and through all, and in all.

ADORATION
Glory and praise to God the Father, the Almighty, the Creator, the Lord of our whole universe. Glory and praise to the Son, the Redeemer, who has removed our fear and our guilt by taking the world's sin upon himself. Glory and praise to the Spirit, our guide and our hope, by whom we are built up in fellowship, knowledge and love. To the Trinity, one God, the source of life and truth and wholeness, be all honour and power and glory from the whole creation until the end of time.

CONFESSION AND PRAYER FOR PARDON
Lord God, your light always exposes the extent of our darkness. Your faithfulness is the measure of our   7/28/85

15

disloyalty. The recollection of your forgiving love
reveals the ugly hardness of our hearts. We claim you
joyfully as our Father, but we do not deserve a place
within your family; for we make up rules to suit
ourselves, and we trade on your forgiving nature. For
the ways in which our lives have worked against your
purpose; and for all the hope you have had for us
which we have not fulfilled, we ask you, Lord, to
pardon us and cleanse us, and receive us back again,
for the sake of Jesus Christ your Son.

PETITION

Lord Jesus, raise us up by the strength of your Spirit,
to fulfil our calling as the people of God. Help us
to approach all our work this week with your values
and with your integrity. Take from us all our
self-centredness, our anxiety, our false pride, our
defensiveness; and help us to love others in the
knowledge of being loved by you, to serve others in
remembrance of your life among us as a servant. May
your Spirit, the Spirit of truth and wisdom and power,
help to use our lives as you would have us use them.
This is our prayer to the Father in your name.

THANKSGIVING

Lord God, we bless you for the gospel of Christ: for
the good news he gave to the world of your justice and
love and compassion. We thank you for the hope we
have of your kingdom, and for the privilege that is
ours in being part of Christ's body, the Church. For
all the friendship and encouragement that we have
found within the Church's fellowship; for the presence
of the Holy Spirit acting in our lives, sometimes in
spite of our obstructiveness; for the joys of home and
family and the excitement of life today, we give praise
and thanks to you, who have planned and given us all
things.

INTERCESSION

We bring before you Father, in prayer, the needs
of the whole Church of Christ around the world.
Help her to hold out to men the way of faith, in all the
changes and confusions of our age. To all who guide
and serve the Church, grant the humility and love
without which no work can be done for Christ.

We pray for our Queen, Elizabeth, and all the
members of her government, that your wisdom may
guide them in their policies and their decisions. And
we pray for the peace of the world—that it may be a
true peace, inspired by the sense of brotherhood within
the human family. Draw us nearer to the day when all
the nations will co-operate against disease and
prejudice and hunger.

Lord God, be with all suffering people: the ill, the
anxious, the bereaved; and uphold those known to us
whose needs we lay before you now. . . . May your
love and your peace reach through to them, even when
we feel powerless to help; and may the example of
Christ's suffering, the knowledge of his understanding,
be a constant inspiration to them all.

For men and women who have laboured through the
centuries to build up the Church of Christ, we give
you thanks. We praise you that our fear of death has
been removed by Christ's own death and resurrection;
and that you, who are the origin of all life, are also
the fulfilment of our lives. Bring us safely to our
destiny, Lord God, by whatever paths you know in
your wisdom to be right and necessary for us. Grant
that when our journey in the world is finished, it may
lead us to that welcome, in the world beyond all space
and matter, which the Lord of life has promised to his
people. All our prayers we bring before you in his

name, our crucified and risen Saviour, to whom be
glory for ever and ever.

Our Father . . .

DEDICATION OF GIFTS AND SELF-OFFERING

Lord God, these gifts have come from you, and we
return them to you as the symbols of our dedication to
your service. May our minds reflect the mind of
Christ, our bodies be fit dwellings for your Holy
Spirit, and our whole life be an offering that brings
you joy and honour; for the sake of Jesus Christ our
Lord.

Service 2

CALL TO PRAYER

Let us kneel before the God who made us;
    for he is our God,
We are his people, we the flock he shepherds.
You shall know his power today
    if you will listen to his voice.

ADORATION

O God, maker of all things, lover of all ~~men~~ *people*, your
presence is with us always, around us and within us.
You are the source of our life, and without you we and
all things would cease to be. You alone are real:
everything else derives its reality from you. Help us to
worship you with mind and heart and all the power of
our being; through Jesus Christ our Lord.

CONFESSION AND PRAYER FOR PARDON

Father, we come to you conscious of the things within
ourselves we hate to remember yet cannot forget and
fear to renounce: our self-indulgences, our prejudices,
our resentments, our hypocrisies, our selfishness. Save
us from self-contempt as we acknowledge these things
and as we remember your love for us in spite of all
that we are and do. Give us the assurance of pardon,
the release and relief of those who know that the past
is forgiven, and the zest and joy of those who know
that the future is still to make. So may we live in that
fullness and freedom of life, which you have promised
that we can share through Jesus Christ our Lord.

7/21/85

PETITION

Lord God, you know how much we need you in our
daily lives and how often we forget you. When we
forget you, do not forget us. Give us strength when we
are overstrained, guidance when we are perplexed,
courage when we are afraid. Deliver us from undue
self-concern, that we may find fulfilment in the service
of others. Make us sensitive to others' needs and
swift to meet them. Save us from fret and tension and
anxiety, that having done the best we can, we leave
the rest to your disposing. And in all things—joy or
sorrow, success or failure, health or sickness—mould us,
we pray, nearer to the image of your son, Jesus Christ,
our Lord.

THANKSGIVING

Lord our God, you have surrounded us with the good
gifts of your love. We remember them now, and we
thank you, the giver. You have given us the gift of life
itself. For the years that are past we thank you;
for the years that are to come we trust you; and for all
the joys and opportunities of this present time we
bless you.

You have given us the gift of love. For our families and
our friends and for all the human relationships that
enrich our lives we praise you. You have given us the
gift of power to control and use the physical world
about us. The good fruits of science and technology
are your gifts for our enjoyment.

You have given each one of us some special gift, some
special cause for thankfulness which lifts our heart in
gratitude to you when we remember it. You have
given us Christ, and through him you have offered us
life indeed, and love and power, for this world and for
the world to come. For this your greatest gift we thank
you from the fullness of our hearts.

INTERCESSION

Father, hear us as we pray for our fellow men, and [*women +*] help us to know our kinship with them as brothers in your family. [*sisters +*]

Break down the prejudice, the selfishness and fear that separate men [*people*] from one another. Help the nations of the world to find a way to live together in peace with honour. Forgive the arrogance of the strong and the resentment of the weak. Bless the work of all those who are bringing aid to needy countries throughout the world, and show us how we must bridge the gap between wealth and poverty, plenty and hunger.

We pray for all those who find the pace and strain of life too much for them; for those who fear redundancy; [*unemploy-ment*] for those who have lost confidence in themselves; for those who are slowing down through illness or increasing years; for those who are over-sensitive to criticism; for those who are overworked and underpaid; for all who are worn down in body or in mind by the burdens which they carry.

Give your help and guidance, Lord God, to all whose work affects the lives of others. Give wisdom and integrity to our leaders; to those who serve in Parliament, especially to those who bear the burden of decision in government; to our industrialists and men [*people*] of business; to our Trades' Union leaders; to all who control the mass media of communication. May those who have power over their fellow men [*women +*] use it with sense and restraint for the good of all and for your glory.

Bless and strengthen the bonds of family life within our land. Teach us how to understand one another better, parents and children, husbands and wives; and through deeper understanding deepen our love. May peace and joy dwell in our hearts and in our homes.

Father, we bring to you now the special needs of
people known to us as neighbours and as friends:
those who are sick; those who are bereaved; those who
are lonely; those who are afraid; those who are
ashamed; and those who are bitter. You know their
needs better than we do. Give them, not what we ask,
but what your love directs.

COMMEMORATION OF THE FAITHFUL DEPARTED
Eternal God, we trust you not for this world alone but
for the world to come. We remember our own loved
ones who have passed through death to a new life.
For their memory we give thanks, and for our
fellowship with them now in your presence. Bring us
at the last where they are, to those things which our
lips cannot utter but which our hearts long for, in the
glory of your kingdom.

Glory to the Father and to the Son and to the Holy
Spirit; as it was in the beginning, is now, and ever
shall be, world without end.

Service 3

CALL TO PRAYER
The heavens tell out the glory of God,
the vault of heaven reveals his handiwork.
One day speaks to another,
night with night shares its knowledge.

ADORATION
Lord God
we come here now
people of many families
remembering different experiences,
but we all come as one people—your people.
In the moment of deepest concentration,
we have known you working beside us;
in the moment of full relaxation,
we have been caught up into your eternal peace;
in the moment of exhilarating delight,
we have heard you laughing with us in our joy;
in the moment of dread and despair,
we have heard you weeping with us in our grief;
in the moment of bewilderment and confusion,
we have felt the steady heartbeat of creation;
in the moment of discovery,
we have glimpsed the frontiers of your truth;
in every thing that matters you have been beside us:
not blinding us with the majesty of your glory,
but allowing us to glimpse the wonder of your reality;
and even when we have not recognized your presence,
still it is only your love that has held us in being.
What else can we do, eternal God,
but open our hearts in song?
Accept our praises,
for we are filled with wonder at your glory and your love.

9/1/85

CONFESSION

We are not, Father
the people you want us to be;
we are not the people we long to be.
Sometimes we reach out for the new life you offer us,
but too often we are content with second-best;
sometimes we glimpse eternal joy,
but too often we are content with passing pleasures;
sometimes we allow ourselves to share our neighbour's
    agony,
but too often we are content to offer cheap sympathy;
sometimes we are inspired to work for a better world,
but too often we are content with self-righteous
    isolation;
sometimes we allow ourselves to believe in your love,
but too often we act as if you were not to be trusted.
Father
this is our life.
We are not satisfied with it;
we long for it to be better.
We know that you will accept us as we confess our
    failure,
and we present ourselves now in the knowledge
of our foolishness, our half-heartedness and our
unnecessary fears.

        (*pause*)

ACCEPTANCE OF FORGIVENESS

Father
we thank you that you have forgiven us
for being what we are;
we thank you that you accept us,
half-hearted as we are;
we thank you that you recommission us,
timid as we are.

Make us now your people,
unburdened by the past, unfearful of the future,
    and joyful in the eternal present;
for Jesus' sake.

INTERCESSION
Father
before we leave the community of your people
we remember the needs of others.
Although we today enjoy our day of rest
there are others for whom it is like other days:
people who must work on Sundays if our life is to
    continue as usual,
people whose responsibilities are always with them;
we pray that even in the midst of their activity and
    their concern
they may know the light of your truth.
Those who today enjoy a break from daily work
must start tomorrow a new week's work:
inspire all the daily life of men
so that we may live together in that community of
    concern and love
that you intend for us,
and work together for the coming of your kingdom.

All over the world today
Christian people have joined to celebrate your glory;
we pray that the Church in every land
may carry that celebration into everyday living,
rejoicing to tell the world of your love,
and to minister to human need in Jesus' name.

All over the world today
the nations and their rulers
remember their past,
contemplate their present,
and make plans for their future:

we pray that a vision of your truth and your glory
may more and more inspire the hearts and minds of
    men
that their rulers may seek only to serve,
and the people may live in peace.

All over the world today
there are people who are suffering—
suffering from illness and pain;
suffering from hunger and poverty,
suffering from loneliness and fear,
suffering from bereavement and sorrow:
we pray
        for an end to their suffering,
        that they may be comforted by the knowledge
            of your love,
        that we may be used to help them wherever
            possible.

Into your hands, Lord God
we commend ourselves, and all the men and women
    and children of the world.
May your will be done, always and everywhere.

THANKSGIVING AND COMMEMORATION
Father, we thank you for everything we have:
for life, with all its fullness and variety;
for all that you have given us in the past,
and for our unbroken fellowship with all your people,
    past and present;
for all that you are revealing to us in our own time;
for all the splendour, as yet unrevealed, that is in store
    for us;
and, above all, for the proclamation of your truth
in the life, death and resurrection of Jesus our Lord,
and for the constant presence of the Holy Spirit,
our guide and our strength.

DEDICATION

We ask, Father, that we may wisely use all that you
  have given,
all that you are giving, and all that you have yet to
  give;
and we dedicate these tokens of our wealth
to be used for the work of the Church,
as it seeks to bring the world to know your love,
that love which calls us to pray together, saying:

Our Father . . .

Service 4

CALL TO PRAYER

God has given us eternal life, and this life is to be
found in His Son. He who possesses the Son has life
indeed. . . . We can approach God with confidence
for this reason.

ADORATION

Humbly and reverently, yet freely and gladly, we
greet you, our God, the living God.
Creator of life, we took our origin from you.
Preserver of life, we gather to seek your sustaining
strength.
Renewer of life, we rejoice in the promise that your
blessings are prepared for us.

CONFESSION AND DECLARATION OF FORGIVENESS

In your amazing grace, most loving Father, you offer
us the blessing of forgiveness.
We acknowledge that we need to be forgiven,
for we have turned aside from the narrow road that
leads to life.
We repent of our shortcomings in faith, obedience, and
brotherly love.
Hear us, therefore, when we pray:

Lord, have mercy.
Christ, have mercy.
Lord, have mercy.

Let us receive from the Scriptures a word of mercy to
all who have sinned:
'As I live, says the Lord God, I have no pleasure in
the death of the wicked, but that the wicked turn
from his way and live.'
Accept then the offered pardon and mercy of God.

PETITION

Lord, you have set before us life and good, and death
and evil—let us choose good, let us choose you, that
we may live. Let us be better today than yesterday,
and better tomorrow than today. Yes, Lord, enable
us to lay hold on life by faith in you, by good works
done through you, for you came that we might have
life ever more and more abundantly, world without end.

INTERCESSION

Lord God, you have given us prayer as a means of
    sharing with you in the task of changing and
    renewing the world. Help us now to pray with faith
    and lively expectation.
In many places the lives of men are still poor, nasty,
    brutish, and short.
Stir, more and more, the consciences of those who
    control the world's wealth, that it may be used for
    the good of all.
We remember the governments and taxpayers of our
    own and other prosperous nations . . .
We remember scientists and technologists, doctors and
    nurses . . .
We remember the agencies for relief and aid . . .

But man cannot live on bread alone: he lives on every
    word you utter.
Empower your Church throughout the world to speak
    your name with vitality and clarity.
We remember ministers and missionaries in their
    preaching week by week . . .
We remember theologians, and teachers of the young . . .
We remember all Christians in their witness to their
    neighbours . . .

In the midst of life we are in death. Awaken in all men
    a new awareness of the sacredness of life, but teach
    us so to live that we may not fear to die.

We remember those who make war upon their fellow
    men, and kill and maim and wound . . .
We remember those who soon will lay aside this mortal
    life . . .
We remember those who prepare the dead for burial,
    and those who mourn . . .

Lord of all the living, remember all whom we
    remember, and forget none whom we forget, for the
    sake of him who came that men might have life in
    all its fullness, Jesus Christ our Lord.

THANKSGIVING, DEDICATION OF GIFTS AND
SELF-OFFERING, COMMEMORATION
Lift up your hearts.
We lift them up to the Lord.

Let us give thanks to the Lord our God.
It is right to give him thanks and praise.

Indeed, Almighty God, we gladly lift up our hearts to
    thank you:
—for your daily care and provision for us; for the
    happiness of our homes and the love of our families;
    for faithful friends and good companions; and for
    every door of opportunity that invites our entrance
    into a fuller life:

—for the love of Christ our Saviour, his life laid down,
    his life restored; for the life-giving presence of your
    Spirit in our hearts; and for the promise, great
    beyond all price, that you will never leave us nor
    forsake us, but will surely bring to perfection that
    good thing which, by your grace, you have begun
    in us.

Unite our thanksgivings with those of the living
    creatures round your throne who join in chorus,
    saying:

Holy, holy, holy Lord, God of power and might,
Heaven and earth are full of your glory.
Hosanna in the highest.

As in joy and confidence we offer our worship and thanksgiving through Christ, so also we present our gifts to be the sign and pledge of the dedication of our lives to the work which awaits us, and we seek the enabling power of your Spirit to uphold and support us in all that we do in Christ's name.

But, before we go, we remember those who, having shared the life of earth, have now entered into rest. Encouraged by the faithful to persevere in the way of Christ, we pray that in the end, with all the redeemed, we may enter fully upon that life which is eternal; this we ask through Jesus Christ our Lord, and as he taught us we also pray saying:

Our Father . . .

Service 5

CALL TO PRAYER

God is near to those who call upon him, to all who
call upon him in truth. He will fulfil the desire of those
who fear him; he will hear their cry and become their
salvation.

ADORATION

We bless you for the assurance that you are now here
with us, our God, waiting to bless us, and to bring to
our living such a sense of joy, and peace, and purpose,
as earth can never give. Yours is a faithfulness that
does not change, or diminish with the passing of the
ages—yours a love expressed in Jesus Christ, at which
we can only marvel. There is no one like you, in
heaven or upon the earth to whom we should go with
our prayers and our praising. So let the glory be
yours, our God, this day and all days, through Jesus
Christ our Lord.

CONFESSION AND PRAYER FOR PARDON

Heavenly Father, our lives and all our ways are like an
open book before you. There is nothing we can hide
from you, and with humility we recall those things in
which daily we come short of the standard set for us by
the Christ. The Spirit of true charity motivates us only
fitfully; concern for ourselves crowds out the
compassion we should feel for others. The things of the
faith seldom occupy the central ground of our
thinking. We live and act as if you were not here at all.

   Have mercy upon us, forgive us all our sins, confirm
and strengthen us in all goodness, and bring us to
everlasting life, through Jesus Christ our Lord.

PETITION

Be now, great God, the Guide and Inspirer of our
lives. Attune our minds and hearts to the Word that
you give for our living. Take from these moments here
all preoccupation with lesser things, that we may find
the answers we seek, and the dedication we need to
live now and always in your glory, through Jesus
Christ our Lord.

THANKSGIVING

Father, we bless you for today and for all that it brings
to us of your love and concern for your creation. With
the light comes reawakening and fresh hope, the
opportunity for new beginnings, and the desire to be
here in this place. You are the Source of it all. In
Jesus Christ all things are become new—and we need
no longer be cast down by the evidence of our
frequent failures. The promise of the Spirit's
strengthening power is ours: and we can thus face life
with gladness, offering you the praise of grateful hearts
and our willingness to serve the kingdom, through
Jesus Christ our Lord.

INTERCESSION

Heavenly Father, you bid us care, as Christ cared, for
all your children, and in his Spirit we offer now our
prayers.

Remember for good our land in these days of unrest
and strife, dissatisfaction and disunity. Help us to find
ways through the barriers we create against each
other. Teach us to see our own wishes in the light of
the crying need of those less fortunate than ourselves.
Give grace and wisdom to those who must grapple
with the weight of our national problems, and re-focus
our minds upon Jesus Christ and his way, that the

quality of our common life may be raised, and we be enabled to see our way forward again.

Lord God, through every generation you have not left yourself without a witness, and no Word that goes forth from you can be void and of no effect. Be merciful, therefore, to the Church of your Son, as it strives now to interpret your will through all the conflicting cries of earth. Strengthen the faith of those who must be strong to endure. Rekindle the fires of the soul for those whose love has grown cold. Confirm with power the resolve of all who falter and are weak, and shake from us all trace of complacency—for only so may we be alive to your presence and your leading, through Jesus Christ our Lord.

Heavenly Father, yours is a compassion deeper than we can ever fathom. In all the afflictions of your children you are there with them, and in that knowledge we pray for all who are overburdened today: the sick, the lonely, the bereaved, the depressed, the unemployed and unemployable, the anxious, and those who are so bowed down with care that they can see nothing that might brighten this day for them. In a moment of silence, Father, we hold them now before you in our thoughts and prayers. . . . With confidence we commit them all to your care, our God, for you are sufficient for all their needs, in Jesus Christ our Lord.

COMMEMORATION OF THE FAITHFUL DEPARTED
Eternal God, you have been the glory, the joy and the hope of every generation. As in life they sang your praise, so lead us to follow their example of steadfast faith and trust; and, when our race of life is past, bring us with rejoicing to the reward of the kingdom, united again with those whom we have loved; through Jesus Christ our Lord.

Our Father . . .

Service 6

CALL TO PRAYER

The Lord is King; let the earth be glad.
Let coasts and islands all rejoice.

You that are righteous, rejoice in the Lord,
And praise his holy name.

ADORATION

Eternal God, creator of all life, the energy behind the vast material universe, we praise your holy name, and we acknowledge you with joy as king and lord. Since time and space began, the whole created order has borne witness to your power and your glory; but ours alone is the privilege of bearing witness to your love revealed in Christ. We worship you, with all the Church in heaven and the Church around the world. Praise and glory and wisdom, thanksgiving and honour, power and might, be to our God for ever and ever.

CONFESSION AND PRAYER FOR PARDON

Lord God, we would not dare to come before you as of right. You are pure holiness, pure love, pure good. We are self-willed creatures, and we cannot even live within the light that you have held out to us. But since, in Christ, you have declared your love and mercy to the world, we come in full assurance of the Faith, and ask your pardon for the failings of this past week. We recall the wasted opportunities . . . . . . the good intentions that were not fulfilled . . . . . . our insensitive speech . . . . . . our lack of discipline and dedication . . . . . . And we repent of any hurt that we have caused, and all the help that we have withheld.

Lord God our Father, forgive us all those sins for which we are ready to receive forgiveness; in the name of our Saviour, Jesus Christ, your Son.

PETITION

Holy Spirit of the living God, raise us up from our past weakness, into the strength and peace of being used for God's work. Do not leave us cleansed and empty; but renew in us a sense of joy and hope and expectation, in the tasks and opportunities that lie ahead of us. Increase our understanding and our sensitivity, until we have a deeper knowledge of the mind of Christ. May his own love inspire our thinking and our speaking; and may his compassion find expression in our actions. We ask this help in his name, to whom be glory for ever and ever.

THANKSGIVING

Almighty God and Father, whose wise, loving providence directs the lives of men, we thank you and we praise you for your great goodness to us. We thank you for beauty and strength and stability in the created world around us; for light, and colour, and the rhythm of the seasons. For the daily gifts of home, and food, and work; for the people who bring us joy; and for all the interests and talents that you have given to the human race, we thank you. But above all else, we bless you for Jesus Christ your Son—our light and our salvation. It is from our life in him that our lives derive their meaning; it is in his truth that we find hope, and confidence, and joy. We bless you for his Spirit with us always, even in the times of doubt and suffering; and we thank you for our membership within the Church, his body. May our gratitude find true reflection always, in the way we use your gifts; for his own sake.

INTERCESSION

We offer prayer, Lord God, for your whole Church on earth; and pray that it may meet the challenges of unbelief and sin, with Christ's own understanding and integrity. Inspire all congregations of the Church in Scotland, so that each may minister with vision to its own community. Be with the men and women who have left home to serve the Church overseas, and strengthen them in the work they do for Christ.

Bring peace throughout the world, Lord God, and justice between rich and poor. Be with our Queen and government, that they may lead our nation in the right ways, and help to free the world from prejudice and tension and aggression.

We pray for all in our community who have the power to influence the lives of others: for parents, teachers, magistrates and doctors; social workers, entertainers, and youth leaders.

Father, may the knowledge of your love be a strength to all who suffer—even those who have received no love from their fellow men. May your mercy touch the lives of those we know, who are ill . . . . . . or anxious . . . . . . or bereaved . . . . . . If our love for them falls short, may they still never doubt your love, or your understanding; through him who suffered loneliness and pain, and even death itself, for our peace—Jesus Christ, our Lord.

COMMEMORATION OF THE FAITHFUL DEPARTED

We rejoice in the great hope we have in Christ, and in the memory of all the faithful who have lived and worked and sacrificed to build up our heritage within the Church. For all the saints who have done great things, and for those who did the small things well and faithfully, we offer thanks. May our lives be a

continuation of their work, and may we one day, by
your grace, be re-united with them in the fullness of
the joy of heaven.

All our prayers we offer in the name of Jesus Christ
our Great High Priest, to whom with the Father and
the Spirit be honour and glory for ever.

Our Father . . .

DEDICATION
Lord God, we bring back these gifts to you, tokens of
our work, our time, our loyalty. May your blessing be
upon them, and upon our lives; and may we be
continually led to see how we may serve you more
effectively; through Jesus Christ our Lord.

Service 7

CALL TO PRAYER
> It is good to give thanks to the Lord;
> For his love endures for ever.

God is love; and his love was disclosed to us in this,
that he sent his only Son into the world to bring us life.

ADORATION
Lord God almighty, creator of the world, and Father
to each one of us, we bless thee and we praise thee, we
rejoice in our knowledge of thy goodness and thy
power. The king of kings knows every one of his
subjects; the lord of lords loves every one of his
people; the judge of all the earth extends forgiveness
even to the most contemptible of sinners. Such love as
thine is far beyond our understanding; but we
recognize in it the fulfilment of our deepest hopes and
longings.

We bless thee for the gift of worship, the link between
eternity and time; and gladly we unite our offering of
praise with the worship of the whole creation, both in
this world and in heaven. Holy, holy, holy is our God,
the sovereign Lord of all, who was, and is, and is to
come—the one, true, living God for ever and ever.

CONFESSION AND PRAYER FOR PARDON
Thou hast not kept thy glory hidden from us. In
Christ, we have been shown the way of consecrated
living; but we are slow to follow it. Father, we
acknowledge our great shortcomings—our mistaken
priorities, our ready excuses, our disturbing lack of
love. We are impatient with the people closest to us,

9/29/85

and indifferent towards those who are conveniently far
away. We do not live up to our own ideals, and our
ideals fall far short of thy truth. We are aware of many
ways in which we have betrayed thee—both by doing
wrong, and by leaving good undone. Thou art aware
of many more, which we in our hardness have not
even noticed.

Almighty God, forgive us, so far as we are ready to be
forgiven, and bring us to new peace and wholeness,
for the sake of him who died for our forgiveness, Jesus
Christ our Lord.

PETITION

Grant, Lord God, that we may take our wrongdoing
seriously, and not just learn to live with it. And help
us also to take thy forgiveness seriously—that we may
go out from here to serve thee in our daily lives, as
people who are indeed forgiven and redeemed. Each
of us has different needs and different weaknesses; but
all of them are met and helped in Christ. Strip from
us all reserve, all insecurity, and all pretence; then
liberate us for the life of joyful, sacrificial service,
which is man's true freedom and fulfilment. We ask
this help in Jesus' name, to whom be glory and honour
for ever.

THANKSGIVING

Lord God, we bless thee for Christ's revelation to the
world; for all that he achieved, and all that he has
taught us of thy nature. In Christ, we see unwavering
devotion to thy glory; in him, we see thine own eternal
love, prepared to give itself upon the cross; from him
we draw our fundamental confidence, and all our
hope for this world and the next.

We give thee thanks for all reflections of Christ's love
within the world—all happy and united families, all

men and women who are moved to work for other people's good, and all who are prepared to brave hostility and ridicule for the sake of Christ and his kingdom.

We thank thee for the great variety of human personalities and gifts; for the skills of scientists and doctors and technologists; the sensitivity of artists, writers and musicians; the qualities of courage and kindness latent in all human souls, which give us inspiration and encouragement. And we bless thee for the great uniting bond of being one family, under Christ. His life and death and saving work were gifts to every man—the faithful and the sceptical, the upright and the lost. For his gifts to the world of gospel, church and sacraments, we bless thee, from whom all gifts have come.

INTERCESSION

We offer prayer for those who seek to do thy will throughout the world, and ask thy blessing on all branches of the universal church. Grant that they may find a closer unity in Christ, of doctrine and of witness; and save the whole church from being static or complacent, when the world has so much need. We pray for Christ's church in Scotland that our courts and congregations may be sensitive to the promptings of thy Spirit. Help us to recognize thy will for our congregation, and keep us in our daily work from cold or formal faith.

We pray for all who still know nothing of the love of Jesus Christ, or of his Spirit's powers; all who can see no purpose in their life; and all who are cut off from thy help by intellectual doubt or troubled consciences. May the Church never be a stumbling-block to them, but by patience and compassion show them the extent of thy great love.

Bless our Queen and all the Royal Family; those who
have positions of responsibility in national and local
government; those who have control over our industry
and commerce; and those who teach the young; that
our society may rest upon right values.

Grant us peace in our time, Lord God, and a new
spirit of friendship and co-operation between nations.
Help people everywhere to make real the brotherhood
of man. We pray for starving and homeless and
persecuted people, and all who suffer through the
greed and ambition of others. May the rich and
powerful nations of the world be shown how best to
share their wealth and power.

May thy love and peace reach all who are going
through times of suffering within our own community;
the sick . . . . . . the troubled . . . . . . the bereaved
. . . . . We pray for the unpopular . . . . . . the
unconventional . . . . . . for those who find human
relationships difficult . . . . . . and for those who
bravely carry secret burdens, known only to themselves
and to thee . . . . . .

May each be helped, according to his need, and led to
find beneath his suffering the peace which passes all
our earthbound understanding.

COMMEMORATION OF THE FAITHFUL DEPARTED
We give thanks and praise to thee for men and women
who have worked faithfully for Christ's Church in
former days: the saints and martyrs and reformers;
those whom we ourselves have known and loved; and
all the great host not remembered now by anyone in
this world. We rejoice that they and we are members
still within the Church of our Lord Jesus Christ; and
pray for faith to follow the example of their dedication
—that one day, by grace, we may join them in the

true, unending worship of that world which is beyond
all space and time and death; in Jesus' name, the
Lord who was dead, and is alive for evermore, to whom
with the Father and the Spirit be all honour and
praise and glory.

Our Father . . .

DEDICATION

Almighty God, we bring these gifts with joy, and pray
that they may be wisely used in the service of thy
church. And, with them, we offer everything we hold
in trust from thee—our time, our energy, our bodies
and our minds—to serve thee this week with a joyful,
total dedication; for the sake of Jesus Christ our Lord.

Service 8

ADORATION
God our Father,
from everlasting to everlasting you are God!
This we believe,
but scarcely begin to understand;
we find your glory too great for words.
Yet we can see your glory:
we see it in the wonder of creation;
we see it in the life that you have given to men;
we see it in the events of history;
and most clearly,
we see your glory in the face of Jesus Christ.
So we can come today,
to join with all your people, past, present, and to come,
and say,
Holy, holy, holy, mighty Lord God,
all space and all time and beyond show forth your glory,
now and always.

CONFESSION AND PRAYER FOR PARDON
Father,
your love for us is without end,
yet our love for you and for one another is weak,
often interrupted by self-centredness, . . . distrust, . . .
    vindictiveness.
Whenever we come together to pray to you,
We have to acknowledge that much of our life deserves
    your displeasure,
        that our life together is too often disfigured by our
        selfishness and self-love.
Forgive us, we pray, and restore us to fellowship with
    you and with one another,
For Jesus' sake.

PETITION
Lord God,
whatever may happen to us, or to the world,
you have put your Spirit in our hearts,
you have called us your children:
so we can turn and call you Father.
Help us, Father, to put our trust in you,
    and to live as the family of your people;
through Jesus Christ our Lord.

THANKSGIVING
Father, we thank you.

We thank you for life:
        for our birth into the world as human beings—
        made in your image, to be stewards of your
            creation;
        for our bodies, and for health, physical well-being
            and enjoyment;
        for our minds and our spirits,
        and all feelings and experiences of joy.

We thank you for life in all its fullness:
        that life which was made visible in Jesus Christ;
        that life together that we can enjoy because of
            him;
        that life eternal in which nothing can separate us
            from your love.

We thank you for lives that have been lived to the full:
        for lives that have been poured out in love;
        for lives which have been inspired to new
            discovery;
        for lives which have helped us to be what we are.

Father, Lord of all life, we thank you.

INTERCESSION: FOR THE CHURCH AND THE WORLD

Father, we pray now for other people, with whom we
share the benefits of your love.

We pray for the people with whom we share most
intimately:
    our families, and our friends;

we pray, too, for the people with whom we find it
difficult to share anything:
    those who hate or dislike us, those whom we fear
      and distrust;

we pray for all the men and women and children who
are suffering today:
    people who know pain and disease, poverty and
      hunger,
    fear and doubt, loneliness and sadness;

we pray for people who govern the world:
    our own government, and all governments, and
      all who are involved in political life;

we pray for the affairs of the world, and the life of the
nations:
    for peace among the nations, and peace within
      each nation;

we pray for the Church of Jesus Christ, of which we
are a part, and for all Christian work and witness.

Father,
inspire by your love all who are trying to serve you;
comfort by your love all who are in trouble;
strengthen by your love all who bear great
responsibility;
create by your love a true sense of brotherhood among
men;
through Jesus Christ our Lord.

Service 9

CALL TO PRAYER
Come, ring out our joy to the Lord: for he is our God, and we the people who belong to his pasture, the flock that is led by his hand.

ADORATION
Above all earthly power, O God, you are reigning. Help us to acknowledge you as king. Underneath the depths of human weakness and sorrow are your everlasting arms: help us to trust in you for all our needs. Beyond the reach of our imagination and desire is your never-failing love and care: help us to realize your presence with us, and to offer the worship of heart and mind and will—all surrendered to your service through Jesus Christ our Lord.

CONFESSION AND DECLARATION OF FORGIVENESS
Though we are bound to you, our God, by many ties, we recognize that in our lives there is restlessness, anxiety and fear. If these arise because we reject your leading and wander from your way, we ask you to give us now the honesty to admit our failings and the courage to repent of them. Hear us, therefore, when we pray:

> Lord have mercy.
> *Christ have mercy.*
> Lord have mercy.

(*pause*)

Be assured, faithful Christian people, there is declared in Jesus Christ, to all who are truly penitent, the forgiveness of their sins, and the renewal of their lives in the power of his Spirit.

PETITION

Lord God, Christ's dealings with our human race have shown the power of love: establish such a love within our hearts that we may love you in sincerity, and for Christ's sake may love and care for all men; through the same Jesus Christ our Lord.

INTERCESSION

We pray you, Lord God, to fan the flame of love in our hearts to give warmth to the words of our lips and thoughts of our minds as we pray for others.

Lord, King and Head of the Church, remember every congregation of the faithful. Strengthen their confidence in your power and will to save the human race, and in the final triumph of your kingdom.

Lord, King of Kings and Lord of Lords, remember the rulers of nations, especially Elizabeth our Queen, her government and all Members of Parliament. Let it be the aim of every government to promote peace and justice, and let the causes of hatred and bitterness be removed from all the troubled places of the world.

Lord, King of all men, remember the industrial workers of our land, and especially those whose livelihood is threatened by economic systems and forces which they have little power to change. When protest is called for, make it strong in its appeal to reason and conscience. And to those who have a measure of power, give wisdom in making decisions and sensitivity in carrying them out.

Lord, King of mercy, remember all who are afflicted— the sick in body, the disturbed in mind, the worried and the tempted, the bereaved, all refugees and victims of war and famine—and give comfort and help, healing and strength.

Lord, King of love, remember all who are closest to us in family or friendship, and be near to all whom we name in silence. . . . May you be known as King, Lord, in every home and every heart, and may the whole earth resound with one cry from pole to pole: Praise and honour, glory and might, to him who sits on the throne and to the Lamb for ever and ever!

THANKSGIVING

Lift up your hearts!
We lift them to the Lord.

Let us give thanks to the Lord our God.
It is right to give him thanks and praise.

Yes indeed, how right it is for us to thank and praise you. We thank you for our experience of the world you have created—for the sights and sounds of every day, and for occasional glimpses into deeper beauty; for the many encounters and acquaintanceships of life, and for profounder and more lasting relationships with those whom we love; and for all that goes to weave the rich and varied fabric of community. But, more than for that, we thank you for the Gospel's joyful sound, for the new light Christ gives to those who put their trust in him, and for the privilege of our commission to speak in his name, to shine with his light, and to build his new community. To the great company of his servants in both earth and heaven we join our voices, as we praise you saying:

Holy, holy, holy Lord, God of power and might,
Heaven and earth are full of your glory.
Hosanna in the highest.

And now most merciful Father, we pray you, through Jesus Christ your Son our Lord, to receive and bless the offering of our worship and our gifts, and so to consecrate our bodies, minds and spirits by the action of your Holy Spirit, the Lord, the giver of life, that we may give ourselves to you, a living sacrifice, dedicated and fit for your acceptance, for such is the worship which we as rational creatures should offer; through Jesus Christ our Lord.

COMMEMORATION OF THE FAITHFUL DEPARTED
And as we praise you for those who have passed in faith from the communities of earth across the stream of death, we pray you to keep us also strong in faith that in the end we may all be re-united in the eternal community of heaven; through Jesus Christ our Lord in whose words we are bold to say:

Our Father . . .

Service 10

(Based on St Matthew 11: 1–9)

This and the following Service indicate another
pattern which can be adopted in the compilation of
prayers for public worship. The theme of the Service
is dictated by the passage of Scripture. Since the
prayers allude to the passage, and, indeed, have their
origins in it, it is suggested that an Order of Service
similar to that outlined below should be followed. The
main departure from normal practice is that the lesson
of Scripture is read very near to the beginning of the
act of worship, thereby allowing the congregation to
appreciate without undue difficulty both the general
setting and the imagery employed in the prayers
themselves. Such a thematic approach could usefully
be employed on Sundays when the theme of worship
is not already suggested by the great Christian
festivals. Moreover, by using the Scriptures themselves
as the source of the prayers—a practice which is by no
means foreign to the Reformed tradition—the
compiler is able to draw on a rich store of imagery
which is at once telling and biblical.

THE ORDER OF SERVICE

Call to Worship

HYMN

Prayer: Illumination

Lesson:

Prayers: Confession
Pardon
Petition

HYMN

Prayers: Adoration
Thanksgiving

HYMN

Words of Authority

Sermon

Ascription of Praise

HYMN

The Offering

Prayers: Intercession
Dedication and Self-Offering
Commemoration of Faithful
Departed
The Lord's Prayer

HYMN

Benediction

THE SERVICE

CALL TO WORSHIP

HYMN

PRAYER: ILLUMINATION

Lord God, Source of Light, Giver of Life,
satisfy our questing spirits
in him who is the image of your glory,
the light which does not fail,
the life which does not die,
our Lord Jesus Christ.
Draw near to us in love
as now we draw near to you in prayer,
that we may be obedient to the heavenly vision
and share daily in the risen life of your Son
both in the worship of our hearts
and in the work of our hands.

LESSON: ST MATTHEW 11 : 1–9 (NEB)

PRAYERS: CONFESSION, PARDON, PETITION

Your servant John lay bound in prison,
no fault attributed to him
save singleness of mind
and great devotion to your kingdom.
Yet by our own wrongdoing
we have less liberty than he.
No walls surround us,
but our vision is confined
and we are captive
to our thoughts of self and personal gain.
There are no locked doors
but those our fragile faith
and fear of risk have closed.

Lord, whose word brought hope to John,
forgive our sins
and give us hope of our release
from prisons of our own contriving.

Lord, we are astonished
by the power of your compassion.
Yet we look on from a safe distance
and withhold the price of true commitment.
Grant that, with arrogance and pride laid low
at your assault upon our sin,
we may no longer evade the issues
and reject the challenge of your kingdom.
Raise heart and mind to heights of hopefulness
at your enriching of our poor humanity.

HYMN

Lord Jesus Christ,
men have reacted to you
in a variety of ways:
shaking their heads in disbelief,
wracking their brains in bewilderment,
shielding their eyes at the brightness of your glory
which cannot be quenched.
In a variety of ways
men have interrogated you:
with Scribe, to trap you,
with Pilate, to test you,
but also, with John, to deepen their faith
and to enlarge their knowledge of you.

Lord, this day we look and seek and ask.
You would have us hear and see
men's deafness and their blindness cured,
as plain disclosure of your divine identity.

Far from a stumbling-block,
you come to us as stepping-stone
to life and to eternity.

WE PRAISE YOU AND WE WORSHIP YOU!

Lord, you are come as Christ,
fulfilment of the prophet's hope,
lighting the gloom of John the prisoner.
After you there comes no other:
yet with expectancy we still rejoice
in all the signs of your continuing presence.
Your blest hands are still imparting
life and hope, where none prevailed before.
We are the poor, made rich
by hearing the good news.
We are singers of a new song,
joining in thankfulness
with saints of every age and race
to bless you.

HYMN

WORDS OF AUTHORITY

SERMON

ASCRIPTION OF PRAISE

HYMN

OFFERTORY

PRAYERS: INTERCESSION, DEDICATION, COMMEMORATION

O God our Father, in your Church
both stillness and vitality abound,
companion virtues in the life of faith.
May all your people be kept
in quietness and confidence of heart,
yet not shrink to serve the cause of right
with vigour and determination
when called by you.

Lord, your Son is come,
bringing, in changed lives,
visible signs of the arrival of your kingdom.
Establish your people's life
not on the easy slogans
and the good intentions
which fertile minds produce
and idle hands let die,
but on active, prayerful commitment
to the mind of Christ.

Remember Lord
all who live simply and speak plainly
amid the complexities of this age:
that, by their style of life
and the directness of their words,
they may set new standards
in a society weakened by indulgence
and confused by twisted speech:
through Jesus Christ our Lord.

Remember Lord
all unjustly imprisoned
for political or religious beliefs,
and all victims of violence or fear.
Give them courage in their plight,
no cramping of their wider vision,
and patience to await
the dawning of a new age;
through Jesus Christ our Lord.

Remember Lord
all of a fickle and petulant frame of mind
who live busy lives
and meet many people,
yet remain unmoved
by causes or by crises:
the easily offended and the hard to please,
those who do not know their own mind,

and those who behave like spoiled children.
Bring them to a new maturity,
deliver them from pettiness of spirit,
and lead them in the end
to share the sympathy and stability
of Jesus Christ our Lord.

Remember Lord
All in our community with charisma,
the power to enlist a following,
to arouse imagination and emotion,
and to thrive on the controversy of public life.
Make them humble and responsible.
And may Christians with much gifts
consecrate them daily in the Apostle's teaching,
that worldly standards no longer count
in our estimate of any man.

Lord Jesus Christ,
we have offered to you
prayer, praise and this money
from the earnings of the past week.
Receive from us also the earnest desire
to please you in worship and in work alike,
and more fully to understand
the cost at which you have secured
our freedom as the sons of God.

God our Father,
reverently and thankfully we acknowledge
prophet's vision,
martyr's courage,
and herald's timeliness
in this and every age.
Remembering John,
prophet, martyr, and herald
who prepared the way for your coming,
we thank you for faithful souls
in every generation,

forgotten by men but remembered by you,
and for those known to ourselves
who have influenced our lives for good.
We are glad that paths have crossed and minds
    have met.
In the fullness of time
bring us all to the heavenly fellowship
of the friends of God;
through Jesus Christ our Lord.

Our Father . . .

Service 11

(Based on St Luke 14: 15–24)

CALL TO WORSHIP

HYMN

PRAYER: ILLUMINATION

God our Father,
your Son, our Lord, has likened
your kingdom to a feast,
and us creatures of a day to everlasting guests.
By the worship of your house
give us a window into heaven,
that we may fittingly respond
to the grace of your invitation,
and sit with you as friends
who taste the joys of your abiding presence.

LESSON: ST LUKE 14: 12–24 (NEB)

PRAYERS: CONFESSION, PARDON, PETITION

All is now prepared,
all, save we the guests,
    save we ourselves.
Invited to keep the feast
we have joylessly stammered our excuses.
We have abused your gift of time
and lacked a vision of our own eternity.
We are a people of excuses
who plead our cause with skill,
while the kingdom is ushered in unnoticed,
    the celebration of new life unsung,
    the bread of life untouched.

Gracious God,
whose Son and servant Jesus
is bearer of an eternal message to the guests
around his table: message of hope and forgiveness,
                              of reconciliation and
                                    freedom;
let us now possess your pardon.
Set us free from ourselves.
Set us free to revel in the festivities of your
    kingdom.

Lord Jesus Christ,
fulfilment of the Law,
yet feeling on your own body
the sharp scourge of legalism;
deepen our love for you,
that we may be disciples in spirit,
and not in letter only,
knowing the true freedom
of those who believe.

HYMN

PRAYERS: ADORATION, THANKSGIVING

Almighty Father,
you have summoned us
to share in the free gift of your love,
to enter the festivities of your kingdom.
Gladly we obey.
Joyfully we keep the feast.
With expectancy we sit at your table.
All is now prepared:
your grace, in readiness from the foundation of the
    world;
your love, acting and reacting down the years.

Your Christ is come to meet with us,
host at the banquet
and servant to the hedgerow guests.
All is now prepared.

SO WE WORSHIP YOU!

O God of the banquet,
your gifts are not the mere crumbs from your
    table,
careless and random in their fall;
but open-handedly and without reserve
your gifts come to us:
    the manna of our daily bread,
    the fatted calf of welcome,
    the wedding wine of renewal.
Nourished, welcomed and renewed
we make our thanks to you,
in words but beyond words,
in deeds but beyond deeds,
through Christ before whom rescued lives
can only wonder, and rejoice.

HYMN

WORDS OF AUTHORITY

SERMON

ASCRIPTION OF PRAISE

HYMN

THE OFFERINGS

Lord Jesus Christ,
give to your Church
clear-sightedness to observe the signs
of the coming of your kingdom.
Help her members to celebrate your lordship
in the arena of life and experience,
and teach them to mark well
their motives,
their priorities,
their conduct,
as those called to be guests at your feast.

Lord Jesus Christ,
the bread of life,
who recognized and, in compassion,
met the daily needs of men,
yet set the kingdom's claims and righteousness
    above all else;
stand with the hard-pressed
in all their daily duties,
that in following earthly aims,
they forget not their heavenly home.
Remember those who seek to justify their actions,
whose lives are blighted by excuses,
and marred by cool response
to human need and to divine glory.

Lord Jesus Christ,
deliverer of the captives,
yet prisoner of priest and procurator;
remember those who know not where to turn,
who stand in the grip of despair.
Give them calmness,
a word to speak,
and a path to follow.

Lord Jesus Christ,
spending yourself on our salvation,
without loss of your humanity,
without the inhibitions of self-consciousness;
help all who are awkward in company
and agitated in conversation
that they may learn the secret of your peace,
and enter fully into the humanity
which is your gift.

Gracious Lord of the feast,
we rejoice that we have part
in the fellowship of the saints
in earth and in heaven,
not through our distinctions or our deservings
but by our acceptance
of your generous invitation.
In heart and mind deck us daily
in the glad garments of your heavenly banquet,
that we see this life,
    its concerns and relationships,
    its work and endeavour,
    its leisure and recreation,
in the context of eternity,
through Jesus Christ our Lord.

Our Father . . .

HYMN

BENEDICTION

II

ADDITIONAL PRAYERS FOR SUNDAY WORSHIP

1. Complete Sets of Opening Prayers

Opening Prayers—1

CALL TO WORSHIP
God is light, and in him there is no darkness at all. If we walk in the light as he is in the light, we have fellowship with one another; and the blood of Christ cleanseth us from all sin.

ADORATION
Lord God, who dost satisfy the longing of our souls and dost fill the hungry with good things, we lift up our hearts to thee. Thou hast taught us to call them blessed that hunger and thirst after righteousness; grant us that hunger, that we may turn from feeding on that which is not true bread to thee, who alone canst satisfy us.

CONFESSION AND PRAYER FOR PARDON
Look on us, O Father, as we confess our shortcomings and sins:
> how prone we are to evil, how slow to do good;
> how easily deceived by the values of the world,
> > and how blind to the things that belong to our peace;

how easily led astray by self-indulgence, and how
slow to practice self-discipline;
how glibly we blame others, and how slow we are
to blame ourselves.

Father, forgive us, for Jesus' sake.

PETITION
Keep ever before our eyes, O God, the vision of Jesus
Christ:
his love and mercy;
his fearless courage;
his firm assurance and faith;
his purity and truth.
Keep us ever close to him that we may be continually
infected by his goodness and moulded into his
likeness.
Keep us faithful and loyal to him; and keep us diligent
in worship and prayer and service.
And forasmuch as all that we have and are comes from
thee, grant us to use all our talents gladly and freely
in thy service.

Opening Prayers—2

CALL TO PRAYER

Jesus said: 'Where two or three are gathered together in my name, there am I in the midst of them.'

APPROACH

O God, by whose power we are continually upheld and sustained, we lift up our hearts to thee as the source of all light and love, all knowledge and truth, all goodness and joy. Help us to lay aside all anxious cares and concerns from the busy world, and commune with thee in this holy place. So may we be fitted to go out to serve thee with a clearer vision and a greater steadfastness.

CONFESSION AND PRAYER FOR PARDON

Merciful Father, we confess with shame how far short we have come of thy will and purpose for us; how far short we have come of what we ourselves hoped to be. Show us clearly what thou wouldst have us to be and to do, and what we must renounce to be worthy of our calling as disciples of Jesus Christ.

Cleanse us from every stain of past sin; deliver us from its evil power, and grant us thy forgiveness and thy peace.

PETITION

O Lord, who hast given us a place and part in the fellowship of thy disciples, make us faithful to our vocation. Help us to put first our loyalty to thee. Save us from putting our trust in the abundance of the things that we possess, but rather make us true stewards of thy bounty.

Give us courage among the careless to be bold to show our concern; among those who deny thee may we be forward to confess thee; and if we are scorned because we dare to follow thee, may we bear ourselves with patience and fortitude.

Increase our faith that we may find our true confidence in thee who changest not.

Increase our hope that we may never be daunted, nor doubt the victory of thy kingdom.

Increase our love that, all fear being cast out, we may ever seek to overcome evil with good: through Jesus Christ our Lord, to whom with the Father and the Holy Spirit be all honour and glory, for ever.

Opening Prayers—3

CALL TO PRAYER
I was glad when they said to me, 'Let us go to the
house of the Lord!'

APPROACH
O God, who hast made thyself known to us as Father
of all, we lift up our hearts unto thee. Give us a sincere
desire to meet with thee; give life to our imperfect
prayers; give us to hunger and thirst after thy
righteousness; and of thy mercy fill our souls with thy
fullness, that we may lack no good thing.

CONFESSION AND PRAYER FOR PARDON
Most gracious God, we confess how unworthy we are
of thy mercy, and of all thy benefits which thou dost
continually pour out upon us. Thou knowest how often
we have allowed our minds to be defiled with evil and
impure thoughts; our hearts have been hard and
unresponsive to thy love; and we have deceived
ourselves times without number and have been guilty
of hypocrisy. We have not sought to love our
neighbour, but only those who love us.

O merciful Father, who hast declared to thy people
full absolution and remission of their sins when they
are truly penitent; grant us true penitence; absolve us
from every stain; and set us free from· the bondage of
evil habit.

PETITION
O Holy Spirit of the living God, come into our hearts
and save us from the snares of our own folly, from the
subtlety of our temptations, and from the tyranny of
our besetting sins. Take up such dwelling in our
inmost souls that we may be moulded day by day into
the likeness of Jesus Christ.

Keep us in health of body and soundness of mind, in purity of heart and cheerfulness of spirit, in charity with our neighbours and goodwill even to those who would do us harm.

And give us the spirit of service that we may gladly give of our time, our talents, and our substance, for the extension of thy kingdom; through Jesus Christ our Lord, to whom with thee, the Father, and the Holy Spirit, be all praise and glory, world without end.

Opening Prayers—4

CALL TO WORSHIP
Jesus said: 'I am come a light to the world, that
whosoever believeth in me should not abide in
darkness.'

APPROACH
Almighty God, everlasting Father, who hast brought us
out of sleep to behold the light of a new day; dispel,
we pray thee, every cloud from our hearts and every
burden of care from our minds, that with a joyful and
expectant spirit we may seek thy face. So do thou bless
us, and cause thy face to shine upon us and hear and
answer our prayers.

CONFESSION AND PRAYER FOR PARDON
O God, who knowest our thoughts afar off, we
acknowledge and confess in thy holy presence our sins
against truth, against purity, against charity. We
confess our restlessness and half-heartedness; our lack
of faith to believe thy promises; our unwillingness to
deny ourselves for Christ's sake.

Grant us true repentance and the assurance of thy
forgiveness, that we may know thy peace and the
blessedness of reconciliation.

PETITION
Rouse us, O Christ, from our apathy and self-
contentment, that we may live as men who are aware
of their destiny and are resolved to finish the work
thou gavest them to do.

By thy humble birth, root out of our hearts all pride
    and conceit.
By thy life of service, give us grace to find joy in
    serving.

By thy compassion for the needy, make us considerate one to another, ever willing to bear one another's burdens.

By thy hallowed and most bitter anguish on the cross, make us to love thee and follow thee, O Christ; to whom with Father and Spirit be all praise and glory, unto all eternity.

Opening Prayers for a Family Service

If you have been raised with Christ, seek the things
that are above.

Eternal God

You were present at the beginning
You hold in being all that now is
You will be there at the end
You matter more than anything else.
You alone, therefore, are worthy of worship.

Although we know this, we have often forgotten you.
We have not been watching for the signs of your
   activity in the world.
We have not been listening for your word to our time.
Even when we have seen and heard, we have not
   always been ready to follow and obey. Forgive us,
   we pray.

In the days ahead help us to put you first in our lives.

Open our eyes to see what is really happening in the
   world, to see what you are doing in the lives of
   individual people and in the lives of nations.

Open our ears to hear what you are saying to us, so
   that we may know what you want us to do.

Give us such trust in the power of the risen Christ,
   that we may seek above all else to do his will.

2. Prayers of Approach

Lord our God, in many places today Christians will be
dancing and singing their praise. Help us to remember
that by the Spirit of God our worship is one with their
worship, and all of us are united with the choirs of
heaven. Holy, holy, holy Lord, God of power and
might, heaven and earth are full of your glory.
Hosanna in the highest.

*   *   *

(AT THE MINISTRATION OF HOLY BAPTISM)
Lord our God, when we look at the sky and its
countless stars we feel the extent of your creative
power. When we see in a mother's arms her tiny baby
we sense the wonder of your gift of human life. Grant
that this day, and every day, something may remind
us that we want to praise and worship you; for you
have made us for yourself and our hearts can find no
rest until they rest in you.

*   *   *

In strength of mind and body, Lord, you have made
    us for your service.
Given speech and song, your creatures rejoice in your
    praise.
Yet we would bless you too in quietness, recognizing
    how gentle is your love.
Father, we have come home to that love.
Jesus, in mercy call us brothers in your love.
Spirit of God, give us love for one another.

*   *   *

Lord God, you are always at work in our world.
Your Spirit brought order out of chaos at creation;
You led your people Israel from slavery to freedom;
You have kindled our love in Jesus Christ your Son.
And still the world is yours, and we are yours,
Yours to grow in grace and live by faith,
    to the glory of your name.
Holy, holy, holy Lord, God of power and might,
    heaven and earth are full of your glory. Hosanna in
    the highest.

*   *   *

Lord,
we are ill at ease
in a world we cannot regulate,
with a God who resists our probing definitions.
Your name comes readily to our lips:
three letters in a book,
but no adequate description of you.

I AM WHO I AM—
that is your Name,
and in its mystery
the too familiar and the trivial
lie deservedly in ruins.
In understanding nothing,
we come nearest to comprehending you.

3. Prayers of Confession

WITH A DECLARATION OF FORGIVENESS

There are five sets of prayers in this section. These are designed to be used over a month, but the first set is particularly suitable for use on occasions when Baptism is to be ministered or the Holy Communion celebrated.

I

General Confession
Father eternal, Giver of light and grace,
We have sinned against you and against our fellow
      men,
    in what we have thought,
    in what we have said and done,
    through ignorance, through weakness, through our
      own deliberate fault.
We have wounded your love, and marred your image
      in us.

We are sorry and ashamed, and repent of all our sins.

For the sake of your Son, Jesus Christ, who died for us,
forgive us all that is past,
and lead us out from darkness to walk as children of
      light.

A Silence

Minister
To all who repent and believe, we declare,
in the name of the Father, the Son,
and the Holy Spirit:
God grants you the forgiveness of your sins. AMEN

*   *   *

2

General Confession
In mercy, O God, grant us sorrow over the sin in our
    life.
We have done wrong, and failed to do good.
We have followed our own hearts' desires.
Our spirits cry out for the right we see in our Lord.

Come down, O Love Divine.

A Silence

Minister
Jesus died and rose again for you.
In humble repentance, take your pardon, know his
    peace. AMEN

*   *   *

3

General Confession
In God's holy presence, we call to mind our many sins.

Father, our sin has brought you sorrow,
has harmed those who share our life,
has been hurtful to ourselves.
We dare not say we have only lightly sinned;
Yet Christ has taken to himself the burden of it all.

A Silence

Minister
In Jesus' name, be freed from the penalty and power
    of sin. AMEN

*   *   *

4

General Confession
Most merciful God,
We confess that we have sinned in thought, word, and
deed.
We have not wholeheartedly loved you;
we have not loved others as we have loved ourselves.

In your mercy, forgive our past sins,
amend what we are, and direct what we shall be.
So shall we delight in your will,
and go your way, with Jesus Christ our Lord.

A Silence

Minister
Hear God's word of grace and the assurance of pardon:
Christ Jesus came into the world to save sinners.
Your sins are forgiven for his sake. AMEN

* * *

5

General Confession
We confess to God,
the Father, the Son, and the Holy Spirit,
that we have sinned,
that we are sinners.
We confess our offences against God and man:
our actions, our words, and our thoughts,
all wrong feelings of soul and body.

In sorrow we present ourselves to you, O Lord,
seeking forgiveness through the cross of Jesus.

A Silence

Minister
In Jesus' name, forgiveness is yours. Glory be to God.
AMEN

4. Prayers of Thanksgiving

I

Creator God, we thank you for the riches of your creation; for the majesty and marvel of the physical universe in which you have set us; for the vast immensities of space and for our small world within it, so richly blessed; for the good and fruitful earth; for science and technology and for all the material comforts with which you have enriched our lives.

Gracious God, we thank you for the riches of your grace; for your unwearied seeking and striving in every age and every place to remake the life of man that human sin has spoiled; above all for your coming to us in Jesus Christ—for the birth of the child, for the life of the man, for the words of the teacher and the compassion of the healer; and, beyond all these things, for the death of the Saviour, for the life that death could not conquer; and supremely for the presence and power of Christ with us now, alive and active in our world.

Praise and honour, glory and might, to him who sits on the throne and to the Lamb for ever and ever!

*   *   *

2

O God, we praise you that you have revealed your nature and your name as Love. We thank you that in love you created the world in all its splendour and beauty, and mankind in all its rich variety. We thank you that in love you redeemed the world from the destroying power of sin and death. We thank you that in love you uphold the world and that no-one is beyond your care. We thank you that in every generation you call men and women to be disciples of Christ so that the knowledge of your love may be proclaimed to earth's remotest bounds.

Accept, we pray you, both ourselves and our thanksgivings as we respond to the generous outpouring of your love.

*   *   *

3

Father,
you have given us everything;
we gather our thoughts now to thank you for your
   generosity.
You have given us life,
and with the gift of life you have given us all that
   makes life worth living, gifts that you have given to
   men since time began:
      the gift of beauty in creation and in the work of
         men's hands;
      the gift of love, and the gift of friendship;
      the continual passing of the seasons, delighting our
         senses,
      telling of your faithfulness and sustaining our lives.
You have given us new life in Jesus Christ—
      the revelation of your love in the life that he led,
      the proclamation of your truth in the things that
         he said,
      the promise of eternal life through faith in him,
      the inspiration to serve him daily through the
         power of the Spirit.
You have given us also, Father,
gifts that are new in this generation:
      new knowledge of your world,
      new understanding of your truth,
      new power to control and direct our own daily
         lives.
We thank you now for all this that you have given us.
Help us, Father, to be your faithful stewards and
   agents in the world; to lay hold on eternal life
   through faith in Jesus; and to use with care the new
   knowledge and power you have given us; so that
   everything we do may be for your glory; through
   Jesus Christ our Lord.

*   *   *

4

Lord God our Father,
we have listened to your Word, and we have thought
about your truth; our hearts and minds are full of
gratitude as we remember all that you have given us
and all that you have done for us.
We come now to thank you for your goodness and
your love.
We thank you for life:
for our birth into this world you have called into
being.
We thank you for our humanity:
for the opportunity to live in companionship with
you and with one another,
and for our capacity to understand and discover,
to invent and devise, to be unselfish and
courageous.
We thank you for all the good things we enjoy every
day:
for food and drink and comfortable homes, for the
love and friendship of family and friends, for the
satisfaction of work well done; for time to rest
and relax.
We thank you most of all for Jesus:
for the glory of God and glory of man in the life,
the words, the self-sacrificing death and mighty
resurrection of your Son our Lord; and we
thank you that he has called us into his Church,
the fellowship of the Holy Spirit.
We thank you, Lord God our Father, for everything,
because everything comes from you.
Father, accept our thanks, and help us to use your
gifts wisely, for the sake of Jesus Christ our Lord.

5. Forms of Intercession

I

Let us pray to God in hope, looking for the coming of Christ to every man.

Let us pray for all Christians, in all congregations, thanking God for the special service to which each one is called.

> Your kingdom come, O Lord;
> *your will be done.*

We pray for the nations of the world,
remembering before God those people especially who exercise
authority for good.

We pray for our own country:
  for its industry
       agriculture
       commerce
  for its education
  for all concerned with healing.

> Your kingdom come, O Lord;
> *your will be done.*

As we thank God for many whose skills are exercised on our behalf, we pray with fervour for help to be given wherever there is need throughout the world.

Let us take our stand before God
    with millions sick in body and in mind
    with the under-nourished
    with untaught people, the ill-equipped and the
        unemployed.

    Your kingdom come, O Lord;
    your will be done.

And let us focus our prayers on individuals known to us,
close to us or far away,
    people who have asked us to pray,
    people who have not asked,
        who would not ask,
        who need our love, in Christ.

    Your kingdom come, O Lord;
    your will be done.

Finally, let us entrust ourselves to God,
who can use our words and actions in his answer to
our prayers.

    Your kingdom come, O Lord;
    your will be done.

*   *   *

2

A PRAYER FOR CHURCH AND NATION

Come, Holy Spirit, come and fill the hearts of your
   people with the fire of your Divine Love.

Father Eternal, send forth the Spirit and we shall be
   remade, and you will renew the face of all things;
   through Christ our Lord.

Let us pray for the world to turn to Christ, its Saviour
   and its Lord:

     for the witness of Christians, in word and action;

     for the Church in Scotland, ministering Word and
       Sacraments in the power of the Spirit.

     Father, your love reaches out to all mankind,
     and you have commanded us to follow your Son
       our Saviour:

     give us grace to do your will, and to share in the
       Church's mission

     to proclaim the gospel of your love to all the
       world;

     through Jesus Christ our Lord.

Let us pray for those who hold office in the nation:

     for Elizabeth our Queen, for the Prime Minister,
       for the Secretary of State for Scotland;

     for all departments of central government;

     for our regional and district councils.

     God the Redeemer, give to us and to all nations
       leaders who discern your purposes; govern the
       hearts and minds of all in authority, and bring
       us on our way to the kingdom of your love;
       through Jesus Christ our Lord.

Let us pray for the world of business:
> for those concerned with finance and investment;
> for markets and marketing, and the people engaged
> in distribution.

> Almighty God, you have placed in our hands the
> wealth we rashly call our own. Give us wisdom
> by your Spirit, lest financial profit turn to
> spiritual loss; through Jesus Christ our Lord.

Let us pray for a Christian life-style:
> for the wise husbanding of resources;
> for less waste, less clutter of possessions;
> for more generosity in helping the needy of the
> world.

Eternal God and Father, you create us by your power
and redeem us by your love: guide and
strengthen us by your Spirit, that we may give
ourselves in love and service to one another and
to you; through Jesus Christ our Lord.

Glory to the Father, and to the Son, and to the Holy
Spirit:
As it was in the beginning, is now, and will be for ever.

AMEN

6. Commemoration of the Faithful Departed

And remembering the communion of saints, we bless and praise you for all who have handed on to us the torch of faith. Give us grace to live by its light and show Christ to the world in our generation, and at the last grant us entrance into the heavenly places; through Jesus Christ our Lord.

*   *   *

We praise you, our God, for those who at any time made known your love and your joy, and who now rejoice in heaven. May we, like them, keep faith with Jesus Christ and receive the reward of the servants of God.

*   *   *

God, grant us all in this mortal life a continual sense of your presence, unity with those who have loved us in faith, and in due time a peaceful death, through Jesus Christ our Lord.

*   *   *

Eternal God, we bless you for your holy ones, humble in faith, who passed triumphantly through earth's trials and now rest in peace. Keep us one with them in faith, in hope and in love, bearing our witness to your mercy day by day; through Jesus Christ our Lord.

*   *   *

Ever-loving Father, we thank you for making us one in Christ with believing people of many generations. Set free in our midst the spirit of praise and thanksgiving, and grant us zeal to serve you all our days on earth, till that time comes when with all the redeemed we see our Saviour face to face.

7. A Eucharistic Prayer

The Lord be with you,
And also with you.
Lift up your hearts.
We lift them up to the Lord.
Let us give thanks to the Lord our God.
It is right to give him thanks and praise.

It is our duty, and it is our desire, eternal God,
Loving Father, always and everywhere, to remember
your love and to give you thanks and praise.
It was your love that made space and time and all the
wonder of the universe.
It was your love that made man in your own image,
calling him to be your companion.
It was your love . . . . . .

(Here may be added a preface suitable to the occasion)

God of love and wonder, we sing your praises:
with the great company of people,
past and present, here and everywhere,
we adore you, saying,

Holy, holy, holy Lord, God of power and might,
Heaven and earth are full of your glory.
Hosanna in the highest.

You are indeed holy, eternal God and Father;
in love greater than we can imagine you gave your
only Son,
that everyone who has faith in him
may not die but have eternal life.

Not as we would, but as we are able,
we praise and thank you
for the reality of his birth,
the glory of his humanity,
the generosity of his life:
for his sacrifice on the cross,
the wonder of his resurrection,
and the assurance that he lives for ever to save us;
for his gift of the Holy Spirit,
for our calling to be his people,
for the hope all men can find in him.

Remembering his life and sacrifice
we now come to his table
as he has invited us to do.
Send to us now, we pray, the Holy Spirit
so that we may be indeed your people,
and that as we share the bread and wine
we may share in the body and blood of Jesus Christ.

And now, Lord God, we offer ourselves,
remembering the perfect sacrifice of Jesus,
and asking you to accept what we offer,
and make it perfect in him.

Rejoicing to belong to the communion of your people,
past, present and yet to come,
we pray in the words of our Lord,
saying,

Our Father . . .

8. Dismissals

Go now, make people everywhere disciples of the risen
  Lord;
and may he be with you always, to the end of time.

*　　*　　*

Go now; proclaim God's word—
You are the heralds of God.
The grace of the Lord Jesus Christ,
and the love of God,
and fellowship in the Holy Spirit,
be with you all.

*　　*　　*

God has accepted your offering in Christ;
go now to offer yourselves,
as God's people,
to the world he loves;
and the blessing of God,
Father, Son, and Holy Spirit,
be with you all.

*　　*　　*

Go, serve the Lord, rejoicing in hope;
and the blessing of God go with you all.

*　　*　　*

Go now to the splendour of God's world;
go to share the variety of human experience;
go to live in brotherhood with all God's people.
The grace of the Lord Jesus Christ,
and the love of God,
and fellowship in the Holy Spirit
be with you all.

*　　*　　*

Go to the uncertainties of tomorrow;
follow where Jesus leads, trusting him;
and God's blessing go with you all.

*   *   *

(*After the Lord's Supper*)

Minister: We have celebrated together—
now let us go to serve our Lord.
People: *We will go. We will serve.*
Minister: The blessing of God go with you all.
People: *Thanks be to God.*   AMEN

*   *   *

(*After a Christmas Service*)

Minister: Return now
to the places of work and leisure,
of tension and release,
of demand and achievement.
People: *We will return,*
glorifying and praising God
for all that we have heard and seen.
Minister: God's peace and goodwill go with you all.
People: *Thanks be to God.*   AMEN

*   *   *

Go now,
enjoy the riches of creation,
share God's gifts with all mankind,
and use wisely all that he had put into your care.
The grace of the Lord Jesus Christ,
and the love of God,
and fellowship in the Holy Spirit
be with you all.

*   *   *

(After an anniversary service)

Hold fast the tradition in which you stand.
Rejoice in God's unending love,
and go to the world
to tell men of his goodness.
The grace of the Lord Jesus Christ,
and the love of God,
and fellowship in the Holy Spirit
be with you all.

*   *   *

Go now,
     enjoy the goodness of God;
     and the blessing of God Almighty,
     the Father, the Son and the Holy Spirit,
     be upon you and remain with you
     for ever.

*   *   *

Go now: you are God's people.
Find your strength in his mighty power.
Take up his armour,
so that you may stand your ground when things are at
   their worst;
complete every task,
and still stand.
And the blessing of God,
Father, Son, and Holy Spirit,
go with you all.

*   *   *

Go, tell the world this good news:
God loves you,
and calls you to walk in love.
And the blessing of God Almighty,
the Father, the Son, and the Holy Spirit,
be upon you and remain with you
for ever.

III

THE CHRISTIAN YEAR

FORMS OF INTERCESSION

The forms of intercession set out below for Advent
Sunday (1) and All Saints' Day (7) might be adapted
to suit the different festivals of the Church's Year; or,
alternatively, they might be drawn up with the regular
service of the Sunday in mind, taking for the theme
the dominant lesson on the day.

Specific forms for Advent and All Saints are included
here merely to suggest in some detail possible
approaches to the intercessory prayer. Ministers will
be able to devise many other varied patterns of prayer
for the intercessions. Wherever possible, these should
be Scriptural in language and theme. In most
congregations the lessons will have immediately
preceded the prayer, and, consequently, both the
words and the content of Scripture will be fresh in the
mind of the worshippers.

It is suggested that the participants (other than the
Minister) should be seated for the whole service in the
midst of the congregation; that they should stand
where they are to take part in the prayer while the
congregation remains seated; but that they should
identify themselves with the other worshippers as
closely as possible, since these are the prayers of the
people and not of a select few.

1. Advent Sunday

Minister: Lord God Almighty,
the Advent Word of your Gospel speaks
to us
of the coming of your Son Jesus;
the Advent Word of your Gospel speaks
to us
of our own preparedness,
of our awaiting his presence to come
among us.
Then teach us, Lord, and all men,
so to order our lives
that we may be fit to receive
Him who comes.

Let us pray that Christ's Coming may
enrich the lives of many.

Voice 1: Christ's first Coming was at His humble
birth in a stable.

So this Advent Sunday we pray for all
young children at the mercy of a
callous world:
children who are the victims of war,
children maimed from road accidents,
children left without the love of
parents and the stability of home.
that the Christ of humble birth may
come to them.

Voice 2: The night is far spent, the day is at hand:

Voice 1: Let us therefore cast off the works of
darkness:

Voice 2: And let us put on the armour of light.

Minister: Let us pray that Christ's Coming may not be a yearly festival only, but a daily experience.

Voice 2: Christ comes again and again in the work we do, the decisions we make, the people we meet, the needs we discover.

So this Advent Sunday we pray
    that religion may not be reserved
      for the first day of the week;
    that men may not separate their
      faith from their work;
    that men may see Christ in the lives
      of others.

Voice 1: The night is far spent, the day is at hand:

Voice 2: Let us therefore cast off the works of darkness:

Voice 1: And let us put on the armour of light.

Minister: Let us pray that Christ's Coming may recall men from thoughtlessness or careless living.

Voice 1: Christ came at His birth, comes daily in our lives, and will come at the end of time as the Judge of all men.

So this Advent Sunday we pray that all men will think of the results of their words and actions. Knowing that we must render an account of our lives, may we use our time on this earth wisely and well, not out of fear, but out of love and reverence for the Giver of Life.

Voice 2: The night is far spent, the day is at hand:

Voice 1: Let us therefore cast off the works of
            darkness:

Voice 2: And let us put on the armour of light.

Minister: In ancient times, O Lord, the prophets
             announced your
             Coming to the people.
             The picture they drew became ever
             clearer:
             Friend of the poor and oppressed,
             Redeemer from sins,
             Man of sorrows,
             Judge of the world,
             Mighty God.
             From generation to generation men
             waited and hoped—
             but now you are with us.

Voices 1, 2: The first Coming is now a reality.
                We are grateful, Lord, for your Coming.
                We are grateful that you have chosen to
                stay with us.

Minister: Glory be to the Father, and to the Son,
             and to the Holy Spirit.

People: As it was in the beginning, is now, and
           ever shall be, world without end.

All: AMEN

2. The Fourth Sunday in Advent

CALL TO PRAYER

Repent, for the Kingdom of Heaven is upon you.
Prepare a way for the Lord; clear a straight path for him.

The stone which the builders rejected has become the
 main corner-stone.
This is the Lord's doing, and it is wonderful to our eyes.

APPROACH, CONFESSION AND SUPPLICATION

Blessed Jesus, Infant Divine, born of Mary in a stable,
prepare our hearts at this season that you may there be
born again. May the mystery of the Father's love come
home to us anew, and earth-born hearts rejoice in
heavenly song. So may we love and serve and worship
you, Lord of Lords and King of Kings, blessed for
evermore. AMEN

As you have called us to repent, be pleased to hear us,
 Father, as we make common confession of our
 faults and failings, our sins and shortcomings.

We have not loved you as we should.

We have not given you the service of our lives.

We have not worshipped you, the Father of our
 Saviour Christ.

Father, forgive us. Bring us again into the fellowship
 of those whom you have called, and speak to us your
 word of pardon: Go in peace. Your sins are
 forgiven; for the sake of Jesus Christ, born to be
 Redeemer of the world. AMEN

Open your word to us, O God our Father, to deepen
   our faith.
Light up its printed page by your Living Spirit, to
   make clear our understanding.
And may grace and truth come to us by Jesus Christ,
   your Son, to renew our trust; for his name's sake.

AMEN

INTERCESSION

Lord God, you loved the world so much that you sent
   your Son; with confidence, therefore, we bring its
   needs to you.

Let us pray for the coming of God's kingdom everywhere.
O Ruler of all, establish your kingdom throughout the
   world.
Make a highway ready for the Lord, so that your Son
   Jesus may come with your deliverance to all
   mankind.
May his justice be done, his good news be proclaimed,
   and all that prevents his coming be removed.

Let us pray for peace in the world.
King of the nations, you sent your Son to be the
Prince of Peace; yet you bring down monarchs from
their thrones and lift high the humble. Lead men of
power to recognize that there is no true peace without
justice, but that in turning to Christ for the answer to
their doubts they may share his victory.

Let us pray for the hungry and homeless.
O Father of men, when the Lord Jesus was in the
world as one of us, he knew the fellowship of an
earthly home, but for three years also he had nowhere
to lay his head. Inspire the hearts of men by the good
news of your love in Christ to feed the hungry and to
house the homeless, that all men may rejoice in you,
their God and Saviour.

Let us pray for our homes.

O Father in heaven, we commend to you our homes and families. For the sake of him who rested in his mother Mary's arms, be with our helpless little ones; for the sake of him who, as he grew, advanced in wisdom and in fervour with God and man, be with our growing children; for the sake of him who was apprenticed in his father's workshop, be with our young people who are setting out to face life's opportunities. May all share in the love of their Saviour Christ; and may they know true joy and happiness this coming Christmas in giving and receiving; for Jesus' sake. AMEN

+ After J's ex. we pray
saying:

3. A Christmas Family Service

APPROACH
Eternal God, we gather with great joy and hope to
celebrate the coming of your Son into our world.
Inspire the worship that we offer in his name, and
make us conscious of his living presence with us; for
his own name's sake.

> (The words in italics may be said by a group, by
> different individuals, or by the whole congregation.)

Hymn 172, verses 1 and 3 (sung by all, seated): '*O little
town of Bethlehem.*'

CONFESSION AND SUPPLICATION
Leader: 'How silently the wondrous gift is given'
. . . . . . We, in the stir and bustle of our
daily life, so often remain unaware of God.

Forgive us, Father,
for not noticing you . . . . . .
for not even looking . . . . . .
for expecting so little of you . . . . . .
for turning away from you . . . . . .

'Where meek souls will receive him, still
the dear Christ enters in' . . . . . .

Forgive us, Father,
our lack of meekness . . . . . .
our pride . . . . . .
our stubbornness . . . . . .
our selfishness . . . . . .

Forgive us all the things we are ashamed of
in our past, and all the ways that we have
hurt you or betrayed you without knowing
it; for the sake of him who was born at
Bethlehem to set us free.

Now Lord, grant to us
> a new beginning;
> *a new hope;*
> new confidence;
> *new joy.*

Make clean our hearts to welcome our Saviour. May
he be born in us, and live in our hearts, for ever.
O come to us, abide with us, our Lord, Immanuel.

AMEN

All sing Hymn 172, *verse* 4:
> O Holy Child of Bethlehem,
> Descend to us, we pray;
> Cast out our sin, and enter in;
> Be born in us today.
> We hear the Christmas angels
> The great glad tidings tell;
> O come to us, abide with us,
> Our Lord Immanuel.

THANKSGIVING AND INTERCESSION

Almighty Father, we rejoice in our knowledge of the
world's redemption in Christ.
> For His Birth
> *His Death*
> His Resurrection
> *And His living Spirit with us*

We give praise and thanks to you, who prepared your
people through the centuries until he came.

We bring to you our prayers for the Church of Christ
now:
> *The world Church* . . . . . .
> The Church in Scotland . . . . . .
> *And this congregation of your people.*

Keep all Christians true to the ideals of Christ, and
fill them with the love of Christ.

We pray too for the world Christ came to save, asking
that peace and goodwill may prevail in it:
>*Peace and goodwill between races*
>Peace and goodwill between nations
>*Peace in . . . . . .*
>Goodwill in people's daily work
>*Peace and goodwill in our family life*

And we pray for the people who have no peace or joy
at this time:
>Those who have no faith
>*The people who have no work*
>Our friends who are ill . . . . . .
>*The people who have no friends.*

Father, bless them all, and strengthen them, and help
the whole world find the joy of Christmas; for our
Saviour's sake, who saved us from despair and fear, and
gives us hope and purpose.   AMEN

DEDICATION

Lord God, with thankful hearts for all your goodness
to us, we bring back to you these gifts; and with them,
we offer you the worship of our lives this week. May
we carry out from here the peace and the goodwill
and the joy of Bethlehem, into the world you love, and
to the people you love—all of them. Through Jesus
Christ, who raises our lives on to a new level.

Our Father . . .

4. Good Friday

CALL TO WORSHIP

I, if I be lifted up from the earth, will draw all men unto me.

Is it nothing to you, all you that pass by? Behold, and see if there be any sorrow like unto my sorrow.

Hymn 243. '*O come and mourn with me awhile*'

FIRST LESSON: ST MATTHEW 26: 36–46

FIRST PRAYER

O Lord Jesus Christ, there was never sorrow like your sorrow, the sorrow which you endured on the day of your Passion. Your soul was sorrowful even to the point of death. Your sweat was as great drops of blood falling upon the ground. But our sins were the cause of your sorrow, and the burden of our guilt weighed you down. You are the beginning and the end of all things, the eternal One, the visible expression of the invisible God. For our sakes you became Man; and in all things you were made like us; that in your heart you might have sympathy with us in our great need and little faith; that you might taste the bitterness of sin, endure its burden, and give yourself up to the worst rigours of its power.

Grant us, Lord, we pray, to have such abhorrence of all evil, that we also may feel with you in your sorrow; make us watchful, that in the hour of temptation we may kneel beside you in the garden of Gethsemane, and not rise till the struggle is past and the choice resolved, to do the Father's will; and give us such willingness of spirit, strength of heart, and patient quietness, that we may not shrink from drinking your cup, nor from being baptized with your baptism. For all our hope is in you, O Christ our God.   AMEN

Hymn 247. 'Throned upon the awesome Tree'

SECOND LESSON: ST MATTHEW 26: 47–56

SECOND PRAYER
O Lord, it was your great desire that all men should
discover the mystery of the divine life; and you served
as Teacher and Guide of those whom you called. You
came to your own, and they would not receive you.
You set your disciples apart to be your companions
and friends, and opened to them the mysteries of your
kingdom. Yet by your own disciple you were given up;
you were betrayed with a kiss; those whom you loved
turned their backs on you and fled; and he who
followed you denied you with an oath.

We also, Lord, have been guilty in the same way; we
have not watched; we have not followed you; we have
been unprofitable and unreliable, and betrayed your
trust; we have aimed at being praised and recognized
by the world, and have lost sight of the true distinction
of being your disciples among men. Light of light,
whom men in their darkness approached with lanterns
and torches: keep us from following the little lights of
the world, that deepen our night; and lead us to that
holy city where the true light shines and never goes
down. Forgive us, bring us back to you, and enable us
so to acknowledge you before men that we may be
acknowledged by you in the presence of your
Father.   AMEN

Hymn 254. 'When I survey the wondrous Cross'

THIRD LESSON: ST MATTHEW 26: 57–68

THIRD PRAYER
Holy One of God, you patiently endured the false
evidence of evil men given against you. You kept

yourself from answering again or threatening them.
You received as the judgement of your enemies the
sentence of death; and you heard it in silence,
committing your cause to him who alone is the true
Judge of our lives.

Grant us, blessed Saviour, to share in the same spirit
and grace; that we may not seek out the honour that
comes from men, nor yet be turned from the truth by
their adverse judgement; and when they shall unjustly
condemn us for your sake, may we endure with
patience. And since we must all appear before you as
our merciful God and our eternal Judge, save us in
that day. For all our hope is in your mercy.   AMEN

Hymn 258. '*O sacred Head, sore wounded*'

FOURTH LESSON: ST MATTHEW 27: 15–31

FOURTH PRAYER
O Lord, the Eternal Word by which all things were
created; by whose command all things stood fast; in
you all things consist and have their being; of your
own will you were given up to the will of others.
Soldiers scourged you, struck you, and spat upon your
face. Over your shoulders, in derision, they threw the
purple robe; in mockery they placed the reed within
your hands, and forced the crown of thorns upon your
head, you, the King and Lord of all. You were taunted
and abused, but you did not answer a word. You
suffered, but offered no retaliation.

Give to us, we pray, the same accepting and patient
spirit: let us never be turned away from your ways
through any mockery or cruelty of men; but be
resolute as those who see the invisible God, who gives
to those who endure to the end a crown of unfading
glory.   AMEN

PROSE PSALM 69: 1–19 (*read antiphonally, with Gloria*)

FIFTH LESSON: ST MATTHEW 27: 32–44

FIFTH PRAYER

Condemned like a criminal, Lord Jesus, you went out to the place of death, carrying your cross; until they took it from you, and laid it upon another to bear, not in pity for your sufferings, but that you might be ready to endure fresh torment. They pierced your hands and your feet; they nailed you to the cross. You were lifted up between heaven and earth, as utterly unworthy, and despised and rejected by all. Even those who were crucified with you mocked and abused you. The chief priests, the scribes and elders, loaded you with scorn and laughed in your face. Of all who had followed you, your mother and your beloved disciple, and the faithful women with them, alone remained beside your cross: no others gave you love and pity, though you showed love and pity for all.

Lord, although we have shared in your grace, our sins have pierced you afresh: we have counted your sacrifice a vain thing; we have forgotten that though the cross of wood no longer stands, the cross abides in the heart of God as long as there remains one sinful soul for whom to suffer. We look upon your sufferings and we mourn. They who nailed you to the cross knew not that they crucified the Lord of Glory; but we have known, and yet have crucified you afresh, and put you to open shame. Lord Jesus, as in your hour of agony you prayed for those who put you to death, so intercede for us also. We wait before your cross. Draw us to yourself; lead us by your example, and help us to take up our cross and follow you to life eternal in the kingdom of your glory. AMEN

PARAPHRASE 44: 3–6 (Scottish Psalter, 1929, Tune: Dundee 51): *'Tis finished'*

SIXTH LESSON: ST MATTHEW 27: 45–54

SIXTH PRAYER

At midday darkness rose up to overshadow the land of your glorious birth and awful death. Yet even in this hour of pain and loneliness you confronted death without fear, confidently committing yourself into the hands of the Father. Such was the certainty of the last word, such the glory of your complete trust, that your death brought to life the centurion's faith, and caused all who stood around your cross to look up to you in wonder and in awe.

Blessed Jesus, Master and Lord, from that cross you looked forward to the joyful welcome of your Father's kingdom. Your life of love is now fulfilled, and yet your ministry of grace continues in the heavenly places, raising us up when we are cast down, enabling us when our strength is low, encouraging us when our vision is dimmed, setting constantly before us the divine life which is our proper heritage. Lord, our knowledge now is partial; but in faith and love we look forward to the day when we shall know you as fully as we are known by you, and see you as clearly as you see us. So in joyful expectation of our entrance into your glorious presence we praise and adore you, with the whole Church in heaven and on earth, now and to all eternity. AMEN

THE APOSTLES' CREED

SERMON

OFFERTORY

OFFERTORY PRAYERS (COLLECTS FOR THE DAY)

Hymn 256. *'Sing my tongue, how glorious battle'*

BENEDICTION

5. Easter Day

CALL TO WORSHIP

(LEADER AND THREE OTHER VOICES)

Leader:	Easter Sunday.
Voice 1:	The beginning of a new week
Voice 2:	The celebration of a new age
Voice 3:	The anniversary of the death of death.

Leader:	The Lord is risen!
Voices 1, 2, 3:	He is risen indeed.

Leader:	Jesus lives!
Voices 1, 2, 3:	For ever!

Leader:	Because he lives—
Voice 1:	We too shall live.
Voice 2:	He has gone to prepare a place for us—
Voice 3:	With his Father, and our Father,
Voice 1:	His God and our God;
Voice 3:	And his presence we have with us always.

Leader:	So this is the day of new life!—
	Blessed are the poor in spirit—
Voice 2:	For the kingdom of heaven is here.

Leader:	Blessed are they that mourn—
Voice 3:	For this day of Resurrection is their comfort.

Leader:	Blessed are the pure in heart—
Voice 3:	For the Lord is risen to be with them.

Leader: Blessed are the peacemakers—
Voice 2:   For this day is the triumph of the
                    Prince of Peace.

Leader: This is the day to give thanks—
Voice 1:   And celebrate—
Voice 2:   And rejoice with all our being
Voice 3:   In the God who made us:
Voice 1:   In the Saviour who suffered for us,
Voice 2:   Died for us,
Voice 3:   And is risen again.

Leader: In the power of his life-giving Spirit, let
                    us worship God.

HYMN

Act of Dedication: before the Benediction

Leader: In the strength of Jesus' victory
Voice 1:   We go from here
Voice 2:   His messengers
Voice 3:   His brothers

Leader: Commissioned to carry his love
Voice 2:   Into every part of our daily life—
Voice 3:   Our work . . . . . .
Voice 2:   Our school . . . . . .
Voice 1:   Our homes . . . . . .
Voice 3:   And our family life.

Leader: Jesus is Lord!
Voice 2:   Not a good man, now dead
Voice 1:   But a risen Saviour,
Voice 2:   Not a figure in a book,
Voice 3:   But a living presence with us.

Leader: We will worship him,
Voice 1:   And serve him,
Voice 3:   And trust him,
Voice 2:   And be guided by him.

Leader: For he is our Lord and our God, in life
                    and in death and to all eternity.

                  Now the God of Peace, who brought
                    again from the dead our Lord
                    Jesus . . . . . .

6. Pentecost

SCRIPTURE SENTENCES
The Spirit you have received is not a spirit of slavery,
leading you back into a life of fear,
but a Spirit that makes us sons,
enabling us to cry, 'Abba! Father!'
In everything, as we know,
the Spirit co-operates for good with those who love God,
and are called according to his purpose.

ADORATION
Holy Spirit, Breath of God,
we praise and adore you
as the creative power of love
at the root of all existence;
we praise and adore you
as the inspiration that fires us
to seek the life God wills for us;
we praise and adore you
as the source of all our freedom,
and the provider of all strengthening comfort;
we praise and adore you
as the bringer of unity and peace,
in whom we love each other.
Holy Spirit, Breath of God,
we praise and adore you.

CONFESSION AND FORGIVENESS
Eternal God,
You give the Spirit that enables us to call you Father.
Yet, Father,
set free, we have continued to live like slaves;
called to work with you, we have preferred to bury
    our talent in the ground;
blessed with the vision of your glory, we have remained
    satisfied with an earthbound faith;
offered the truth of your Gospel, we have clung to the
    half truths that comfort us;
invited into your light, we have stayed in the shadows.
Yet you are our Father still.
In never-ending love, you forgive us, if only we will
    turn to you and seek you.
We praise and thank you, Father,
for your compassion and forgiveness
in Jesus Christ our Lord.

SUPPLICATION
God, give us courage to exist in you:
to bear our rule of forgiveness, mercy and compassion
through dread and terror and terror's doubt,
daring to return good for evil
without thought of what will come.
God, give us courage to exist in you,
and let our flesh be welcome to creation.

INTERCESSION
Father, your Holy Spirit teaches us that
there is no life that is not in community,
and no community not lived in praise of God.

As members of the community of the Church,
we pray that it may be faithful,
and have the strength to do your will.

As members of the community of the nation,
we pray that it may be a nation and a people
inspired by justice and compassion,
and that our rulers may be guided and strengthened
    by the Holy Spirit
to lead us in the way of truth.

As members of the community of mankind, humankind
we pray that the nations may live together in peace,
that the strong may help the weak,
    and the rich may help the poor,
that all who are ill or in pain,
    lonely or sad, may find relief,
and that all who work for the good of others
may know that they are doing your will.

As we remember our membership in these wider
    communities
we remember that we also belong to smaller
    communities:
this congregation,
this town,
the communities of work and leisure,
the family community of those we love most dearly;
and we pray that in all these
we may live as the Spirit prompts us to live,
caring for one another and forgiving one another
for Jesus' sake.

Father, your Holy Spirit teaches us that
there is no life that is not in community,
and no community not lived in praise of God.

May all these communities praise you,
and may your will be done,
Always and everywhere.

THANKSGIVING AND DEDICATION

We thank you, Father,
not only for all that we have,
but also for all that we long for.

We thank you that you have given us so much,
but also that you do not leave us satisfied.

We thank you that your Holy Spirit
is always awakening us to new truths and insights,
inspiring us to new adventures and enterprises,
and arousing in us increasing desire for all
    that you mean us to have.

In Jesus Christ, you have made available to us
more than we can ask or think.
We thank you for the inexhaustible riches of your
    goodness,
and for the incredible wonder of your promises.

As we speak our thanks
we offer our gifts of money for the work of your
    kingdom,
and ourselves to co-operate with your Holy Spirit.
Accept it all, Father, and make it perfect,
for Jesus' sake.

7. All Saints' Day

INTERCESSIONS

Minister:	In our prayers for others on this [Sunday after] All Saints' Day, we remember especially all who belong with us to the whole family of God's people.
Voice 1:	Who are the saints?
Voices 2, 3:	We are the saints.
Voice 1:	All of us?
Voices 2, 3:	Yes, all of us!
Voice 1:	The living, too?
Voices 2, 3:	The living and the dead: one family in heaven and on earth.
Voice 1:	What makes us saints?
Voice 2:	Our baptism.
Voice 3:	Our belonging to the Church.
Voice 2:	Our faith in Christ.
Voice 1:	And our goodness, too?
Voices 2, 3:	God's goodness, not ours!
Voice 2:	All saints are forgiven sinners.
Voice 3:	Forgiven sinners are all saints.
Voice 1:	Saints and sinners:
Voice 2:	Sinners and saints.
Voice 3:	Love and forgiveness:
Voice 1:	Forgiveness and love
Voice 2:	Heaven and earth:
Voice 3:	Earth and heaven.
Voice 1:	Past and present:
Voice 2:	Present and past.

Minister: Let us pray

Voice 1:   With Peter
Voices 2, 3:   Give us faith like a rock.

Voice 1:   With Andrew
Voices 2, 3:   Help us to bring men to Christ.

Voice 1:   With John the Baptist
Voices 2, 3:   Show us your kingdom in the affairs of men.

Voice 1:   With Mary Magdalene
Voices 2, 3:   Give us a flair for gracious deeds.

Voice 1:   With John, the Beloved Disciple
Voices 2, 3:   Bring us to love our Master.

Voice 1:   With Thomas
Voices 2, 3:   Grant that we may cry, 'My Lord and my God!'

Minister: Now let us pray for those who make up the communion of saints.

Voice 1:   Let us pray for all baptized Christians [especially for the little child to be baptized here].

Minister: Lord, hear us.
People: *Lord, graciously hear us.*

Voice 2:   Let us pray for all who belong to the church of Christ, especially for all our fellow-Christians in this congregation.

Minister: Lord, hear us.
People: *Lord, graciously hear us.*

Voice 3:   Let us pray for all whose faith in Christ
                is growing and maturing, that they may
                see its meaning for their lives.

Minister: Lord, hear us.
People: *Lord, graciously hear us.*

Voice 1:   And let us give thanks for all Christians
                of other ages and of other lands who,
                with us, make up the communion of
                saints.

Minister: Glory be to the Father, and to the Son,
                and to the Holy Spirit:
People: *As it was in the beginning, is now, and ever
                shall be, world without end.*
All: AMEN

IV

THEMATIC PRAYERS

1. The Word of God

A voice from God comes: 'This is my Son, the Beloved. Listen to Him.'

Ever present God, all the time you are trying to speak to us.
You speak to us through the happenings in the world.
You speak to us through the words and actions of others.
Above all, you speak to us through the earthly life of Jesus.

Forgive us that so often we are deaf to what you are saying to us.
At times we are deaf because our ears are filled with other voices.
At times we are deaf because we are afraid of the challenge you may offer to us.
At times we are deaf because we fear your rebuke.

Yet we know that we have no need to fear.
You are always speaking to us the word of acceptance and forgiveness.
Help us to hear and accept that word.
You are always offering help to fulfil any work which you have given us to do.
Help us to hear that word of encouragement.
You can give us the clue to full living.
Help us to hear and accept that word of inspiration.

2. The Presence of Jesus

'As the Father hath sent me, so send I you.'

Lord Jesus, we remember that you chose men and
women to share in your work.
You challenged them to carry on with your work when
you were no longer present in the flesh.
You promised them your power and strength and
courage.
You have chosen us to worship you in church and also
to work with you in the world.

Too often we have failed to recognize the work you
are doing.
Too often we have compromised with what is wrong.
Too often we have not championed the needs of those
who are unjustly treated.
Too often we have been afraid to take risks, fearing
failure, forgetting your power to help.

Lord, help us in the days ahead to work with you, in
whatever you are doing in the world.
Open our eyes to know what it is.
Give us both love and courage to act.

3. Joy

'Rejoice in the Lord, and again I say "rejoice!"'

We rejoice today in the beauties of the world which
   you have made.
We rejoice today in the living presence of Jesus in our
   midst.
We rejoice that he is still active in the world.
We rejoice that we have seen so many signs of his
   Spirit in the lives of those around us.

Forgive us when we take this world for granted.
Forgive us when our faith is so weak that we do not
   expect our prayers to be answered.
Forgive us when we allow ourselves to get depressed. *discouraged + angry*

Open our eyes that we may not miss the beauties of
   the world. *+ your grace*
Open our eyes to see the goodness in others, especially
   when we are tempted to condemn.
Then give us grateful hearts that we may rejoice, and
   sing your praise.

4. Courage

'Be strong, let your heart be bold, all you who hope
   in the Lord.'

Lord Jesus, we remember your courage in standing up
   for the right in the face of opposition.
We remember your care for all who were unjustly
   treated.
We remember your welcome for all who were outside
   the people of God.

Forgive our many fears.
Forgive us that we are so often blind to injustice in the
   world because we do not sufficiently care.
Forgive us that we miss so many opportunities of
   making the lives of others easier.
Forgive us that we are so slow to welcome strangers
   while so anxious to feel at ease ourselves.

Give us greater courage.
Convince us that if we will only stand for the right,
   you will give us the strength we need.
Widen our love that we may be able to help strangers
   be at home in your family.

5. Unity

Jesus prayed: 'Neither pray I for these alone, but for
   them also which shall believe on me through their
   word that they all may be one; that the world may
   believe that Thou hast sent me.'

Father, we are glad today that you sent Jesus to draw
   together all men and women into one family.
We are glad that through our baptism you have
   brought us into that family.
We are glad that you are inspiring men and women to
   work for the visible unity of your family which
   appears to be divided.

Jesus, we are sorry that we are separated from others
   who are also your brothers.
We are not fully united even with those who share our
   home, who live in our streets, or who work beside us.
We do not make as much effort as we might to
   understand people of other races and colours who do
   not have the same customs as we have.
We have not done as much as we could have done to
   unite with members of other churches.

Holy Spirit, deliver us from taking for granted the
   divisions in the world, divisions between East and
   West, divisions between black and white, divisions
   between the churches.

Help us to understand those who are different from us.
Open our eyes to see truth, which others have but to
   which we are at the moment blind.
In your Church gather us together as one family, that
   all may see that we are one, and so believe.

6. In Time of Depression

Lord Jesus,
Your love for us inspired you to leave all the comfort
    and security of home;
Your love led you to reach out to the lost and the
    disreputable, ignoring hostile looks;
Your love transcended all tradition and all law.
It enabled you to face injustice, misunderstanding,
    death.

Our love is not strong enough to embrace hardship.
        Father, forgive us.
Our love is not prepared to face the ridicule and the
    misunderstanding of other people.
        Father, forgive us.
Our love too easily acknowledges defeat when things
    go wrong.
        Father, forgive us.

In the days ahead, when we are threatened with
    failure, give us vision to discover your will, and
    courage to fulfil it.
Give us strength to persevere, and sure faith in the
    final victory of Jesus Christ our Lord.

7. Freedom

'If you continue in my word, you are truly my
   disciples, and you will know the truth, and the truth
   will make you free.'

Lord Jesus, you are truly free.
You have offered us your freedom but we have lacked
   the courage to accept it.
Lead us into the freedom that your truth makes
   possible.

On earth you were free from the fear of what others
   were thinking.
Often we are afraid to say what we think, or to do
   what we ought, because we fear what others may
   think about us.
You were free to accept people for themselves, and
   not just as members of groups.
This we find hard to do, and often judge others
   unjustly because of the company they keep.

You were free from the wish to amass earthly goods
   and so were ready to leave your home, and to
   depend on others for food and shelter.
In our burning desire to achieve independence, we
   wrongly rely on the things we possess.

Secure in the knowledge of your Father's love, you
   were free from the need to assert your own
   importance.
When someone called you good, you turned him away
   from praising you to praising the Father.
We so often look for praise and recognition for
   ourselves.

Release us from the burden of our failures and give us
    the same freedom that you enjoyed on earth.
Help us to treat all men as neighbours, whether or not
    they are of the same colour; whether or not they
    belong to our nation; whether or not they share our
    political views.
Help us to live our own lives without the fear of what
    others think about us.
Set us free from the blind pursuit of material gain.
Above all, so help us to experience your love for us
    that we do not need to seek for the recognition and
    praise of men, but may know that love is all that
    matters in the end.

8. Trust and Obedience

Jesus said: 'In truth, in very truth, I tell you, he who
has faith in me will do what I am doing; and he will
do greater things still because I am going to the
Father. Indeed, anything you ask in my name I
will do.'

Ever present God, we remember your unfailing love
for us.
However much we forget, you never fail to remember us.
However often we prefer our own will to your will,
you go on loving us.
However many of our friends give us up, you go on
believing in us.
Your love for us was so great that you were ready to
send Jesus to us.

Ever present God, we confess today that we do not
return your love.
We are unwilling to give up the things we want, even
when they hinder us from doing your will.
Forgetting your power to help, we do not attempt to
serve you when the way seems hard.

Ever present God, help us, as we experience your love
for us,
to show our love for you by living as you mean us to live.
Give us such trust in your power, and in your will to
help us,
that we take risks in your service.
Remind us of your power to help not only us, but all
those whom we love.

Ever present God, remind us of your constant presence;
Inspire in us faith and trust;
Help us, through faith, to obey,
And to do the things that Jesus did.

9. 'Lead us not into Temptation'

The Lord says: 'My grace is all you need.'

Eternal God,
you have brought us through many experiences into
　　your presence.
May we find here all that we need.
Our hearts are restless until they find their rest in you.
Our wills are divided until we are at one with you.
Our wisdom fails until we are inspired by you.
Our strength is wasted until we do your will.
Gather us together,
and by your grace give us peace, unity, and purpose.
We ask it because you have called us by Jesus Christ.

In our dealings with people whom we might despise;
in the hour of success, when we might take the glory
　　to ourselves;
when tempted to pride;
Lord, give us humility, by your grace.

When challenged to befriend those who do not attract us;
when challenged to alter our plans;
when tempted to self-centredness;
Lord, give us an open heart and mind, by your grace.

When following Christ may lead to derision, suffering,
　　or sacrifice;
when the future seems uncertain;
when we are challenged to risk and experiment;
when tempted to fear;
Lord, give us courage, by your grace.

When our plans fail;
when we suffer disaster;
when we know pain and sickness;
when tempted to self-pity;
Lord, give us strength, by your grace.

As we face life day by day,
whatever may come,
in all temptation,
Lord, give us your grace.